Wiley

2018

CPAexcel®
EXAM REVIEW
FOCUS NOTES

Wiley
2018 CPAexcel®
EXAM REVIEW
FOCUS NOTES

FINANCIAL ACCOUNTING AND REPORTING

WILEY

CONTENTS

v

Contents   **vi**

PREFACE

This publication is a comprehensive yet simplified study program. It provides a review of all the basic skills and concepts tested on the CPA exam and teaches important strategies to take the exam faster and more accurately. This tool allows you to take control of the CPA exam.

This simplified and focused approach to studying for the CPA exam can be used:

- As a handy and convenient reference manual
- To solve exam questions
- To reinforce material being studied

Included is all of the information necessary to obtain a passing score on the CPA exam in a concise and easy-to-use format. Due to the wide variety of information covered on the exam, a number of techniques are included:

- Acronyms and mnemonics to help you learn and remember a variety of rules and checklists
- Formulas and equations that simplify complex calculations required on the exam
- Simplified outlines of key concepts without the details that encumber or distract from learning the essential elements

- Techniques that can be applied to problem solving or essay writing, such as preparing a multiple-step income statement, determining who will prevail in a legal conflict, or developing an audit program
- Pro forma statements, reports, and schedules that make it easy to prepare these items by simply filling in the blanks
- Proven techniques to help you become a smarter, sharper, and more accurate test taker

This publication may also be useful to university students enrolled in Intermediate, Advanced, and Cost Accounting classes; Auditing, Business Law, and Federal Income Tax classes; or Economics and Finance classes.

FINANCIAL ACCOUNTING STANDARDS BOARD (FASB)

FASB and Standard Setting

Organizations

Financial Accounting Standards Board (FASB)

Private sector body that establishes Generally Accepted Accounting Principles (GAAP)

- Financial Accounting Foundation (FAF)—appoints members of FASB and provides funding
- Financial Accounting Standards Advisory Council (FASAC)—Provides guidance on policy, priorities, etc.

Organizations (continued)

Securities and Exchange Commission (SEC)

- Relinquished authority to establish GAAP to FASB
- Enforcement authority

American Institute of Certified Public Accountants (AICPA)

- National professional organization for practicing CPAs

Private Company Council (PCC)

- Private companies (Little GAAP)

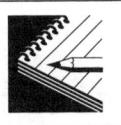

External Financial Report

The financial (annual) report is prepared by applying (GAAP) and contains the following key components:

1. Income Statement—entity performance for the period
2. Statement of Comprehensive Income—reports all non-owner changes in equity for the period; includes net income (or loss) and items included in comprehensive income that are not part of net income
3. Balance Sheet—financial position at reporting date
4. Statement of Stockholders' Equity—changes in the owners' equity for the period
5. Statement of Cash Flows—describes major changes in cash (including restricted cash) by meaningful category
6. Footnote Disclosures and supplementary schedules
7. Auditor's Opinion

Elements of Financial Statements

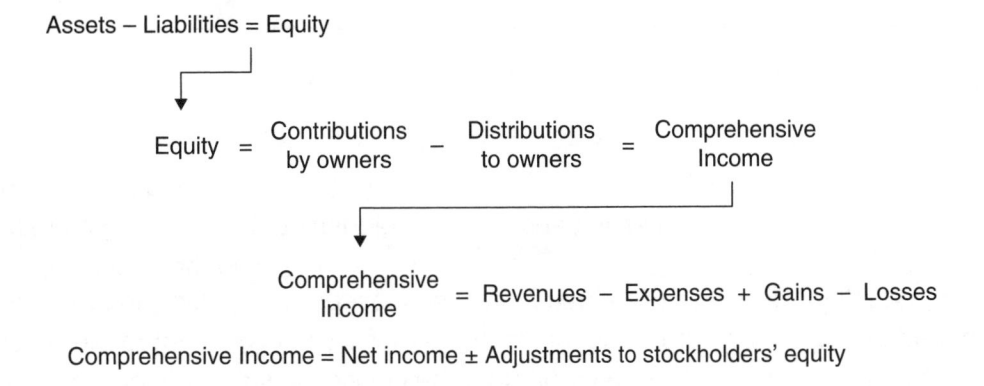

Assets – Liabilities = Equity

Equity = $\dfrac{\text{Contributions}}{\text{by owners}}$ – $\dfrac{\text{Distributions}}{\text{to owners}}$ = $\dfrac{\text{Comprehensive}}{\text{Income}}$

$\dfrac{\text{Comprehensive}}{\text{Income}}$ = Revenues – Expenses + Gains – Losses

Comprehensive Income = Net income ± Adjustments to stockholders' equity

Financial statements are designed to meet the objectives of financial reporting

Accrual Accounting

Financial Statements reflect accrual basis of accounting

Deferrals:

Cash activity occurs before recognition of revenue or expense

- Expenses—prepaid
- Revenues—unearned

Accruals

Economic event occurs before cash is received or paid

- Expenses—accrued
- Revenues—receivable

Revenue Items

Event	Account created	Examples
Cash received before revenue occurs (deferral)	Deferred revenue—liability	Rent, subscriptions, gift cards Dr: Deferred Account; Cr: Revenue
Revenue occurs before cash received (accrual)	Accrued asset—asset	Sales on account, interest, rent Dr: Receivable; Cr: Revenue

Expense Items

Event	Account created	Examples
Cash paid before expense incurred (deferral)	Deferred expense—asset	Prepaid insurance, supplies, rent, PP&E Dr: expense; Cr: prepaid item or A/D
Expense incurred before cash paid (accrual)	Accrued expense—liability	Salaries, wages, interest, taxes Dr: expense; Cr: payable

Deferral Example—Prepaid Insurance

Prepaid insurance (end of year)

    Total premiums paid $\times$ (Months remaining / Total # of months)

Insurance expense

    Prepaid insurance (beginning) + Premiums paid – Prepaid insurance (ending)

or

    Total premiums paid $\times$ (Months in period / Total # of months)

    Adjusting journal entry:

Dr: Insurance Expense   xxx

    Cr: Prepaid Insurance   xxx

Converting from Cash Basis to Accrual Basis

Revenues

Cash (amount received)	xx	
Increase in accounts receivable (given)	xx	
Decrease in accounts receivable (given)		xx
Revenues (plug)		xx

Cost of Sales

Cost of sales (plug)	xx	
Increase in inventory (given)	xx	
Decrease in accounts payable (given)	xx	
Decrease in inventory (given)		xx
Increase in accounts payable (given)		xx
Cash (payments for merchandise)		xx

Expenses

Expense (plug)	xx	
Increase in prepaid expenses (given)	xx	
Decrease in accrued expenses (given)	xx	
Decrease in prepaid expenses (given)		xx
Increase in accrued expenses (given)		xx
Cash (amount paid for expense)		xx

Objectives and Qualitative Characteristics of Financial Reporting

Objectives of financial reporting are to provide useful information about the entity to current and future investors and creditors.

Useful information includes:

- Information about the amount, timing, and uncertainty of an entity's cash flows
- Information about the reporting entity's economic resources and claims against those resources
- Changes in those economic resources and claims
- Information about the ability of the entity to generate future net cash inflows
- Information about the effectiveness with which management has met its stewardship responsibilities

Qualitative Characteristics of Accounting Information

Primary Users of Accounting Information

Existing and Potential Investors, Lenders, and Other Creditors

Pervasive Constraint

Benefits > Costs

Decision Usefulness

Fundamental Qualitative Characteristics

Relevance ⟷ Faithful Representation

- Predictive Value
- Confirmatory Value

- Complete
- Neutral
- Free from Error

Enhancing Qualitative Characteristics

- Comparability (consistency helps achieve comparability)
- Verifiability
- Timeliness
- Understandability

Threshold for Recognition

Materiality
(Entity-specific and related to relevance)

Focus on

Financial Accounting Standards Board (FASB)

12

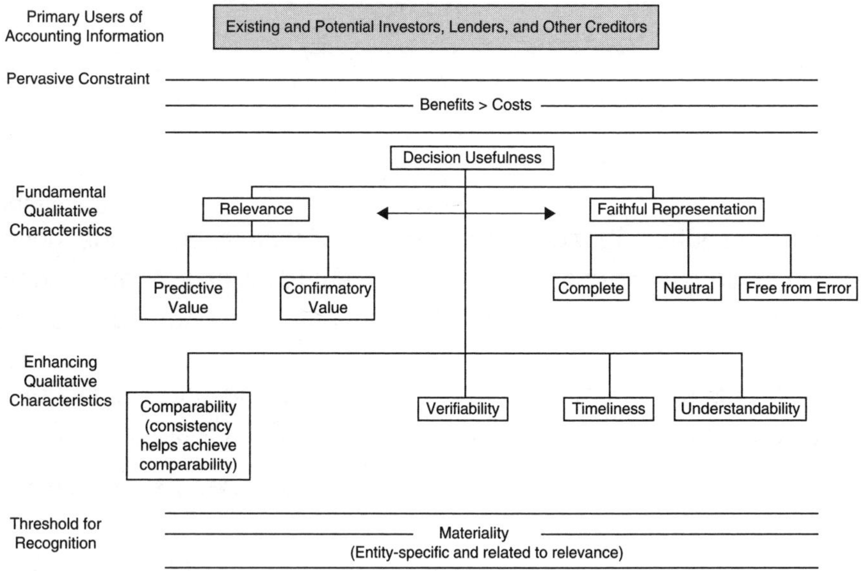

Accounting Assumptions and Principles

Assumptions

- Entity assumption
- Going-concern assumption
- Unit-of-measure assumption
- Time period assumption

Principles

- Revenue recognition
- Expense recognition
- Measurement
- Full disclosure

Fair Value Concepts

Fair value (FV)—The price that would be received to sell an asset or paid to transfer a liability in an orderly transaction between market participants at the measurement date (exit price) under current market conditions

Principal market (greatest volume of activity)

Most advantageous market (maximizes selling price received or minimizes transfer price)

Highest and best use—Maximize the value of the asset or group of assets

Valuation techniques (approaches to determine FV)

> Market approach—Uses prices generated by real market transactions

> Income approach—Discounts future amounts to a current present value

> Cost approach—Current replacement cost

Net asset value (NAV) as practical expedient (allowed when there is no readily determinable fair value and investee reports net assets value at fair value

Fair Value Option

- May be applied instrument by instrument, with a few exceptions, such as investments otherwise accounted for by the equity method
- Is irrevocable
- Is applied only to entire instruments and not to portions of instruments

Available for

- Recognized financial assets and financial liabilities with the following major exceptions:
    - An investment in a subsidiary that the entity is required to consolidate
    - Pension and other postretirement benefit plans including employee stock plans
    - Lease assets and liabilities
    - Deposit liabilities of banks, savings and loan associations, credit unions, etc.
- Firm commitments that would otherwise not be recognized at inception and that involve only financial instruments

Fair Value Option (continued)

- Nonfinancial insurance contracts and warranties that the insurer can settle by paying a third party to provide those goods or services
- Host financial instruments resulting from separation of an embedded nonfinancial derivative instrument from a nonfinancial hybrid instrument

Recognize unrealized gains and losses in earnings for businesses and in statement of activities for nonprofit organizations

Fair Value Measurements

Six-step application process

1. Identify asset or liability to measure
2. Determine principle or advantageous market
3. Determine valuation premise
4. Determine valuation technique
5. Obtain inputs (levels)
6. Calculate fair value

Multiple disclosures for assets/liabilities measured at fair value on a recurring/nonrecurring basis

Fair Value Hierarchy

Fair value hierarchy (level 1, 2, and 3 inputs)

> Level 1—Quoted prices in active markets for identical assets or liabilities

> Level 2—Inputs such as quoted prices on similar assets or liabilities or observable for the asset or liability, such as interest rates and yield curves

> Level 3—Unobservable inputs for the asset or liability that reflect the reporting entity's own assumptions about the assumptions that market participants would use in pricing the asset or liability (including assumptions about risk)

Fair value option—An election to value certain financial assets and financial liabilities at fair value is available. Entities may not elect to measure certain items, such as investments in entities to be consolidated, lease-related assets or liabilities, etc.

Note: If NAV is used as practical expedient, it is not classified into the fair value hierarchy, disclosures are required

INTERNATIONAL FINANCIAL REPORTING STANDARDS (IFRS)

International Accounting Standards Board (IASB) establishes IFRS

- Principles-based standards
- IFRS hierarchy

IFRS Elements

- Assets
- Liabilities
- Equity
- Income (includes both revenues and gains)
- Expense (includes expenses and losses)

IFRS and U.S. Conceptual Framework as Converged

Fundamental Characteristics/Decision Usefulness

Relevance
- Predictive value
- Feedback/confirmatory value
- Materiality

Faithful Representation
- Completeness
- Neutrality
- Free from error

Enhancing Characteristics
- Comparability
- Verifiability
- Timeliness
- Understandability

Constraints
- Benefit versus costs

IFRS Statement of Financial Position Format

- Noncurrent assets
- Current assets
- Equity
- Noncurrent liabilities
- Current liabilities

Emphasizes the long-run perspective

IFRS Income Statement—Statement of Comprehensive Income

The following items are required to be reported on the face of the statement of comprehensive income:

- Revenue (referred to as income)
- Finance costs (interest expense)
- Share of profits and losses of associates and joint ventures accounted for using equity method
- Tax expense
- Discontinued operations
- Profit or loss
- Each component of other comprehensive income
- Share of other comprehensive income of associates under the equity method
- Total comprehensive income

No extraordinary items under IFRS (like GAAP)

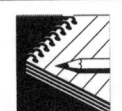

GENERAL-PURPOSE FINANCIAL STATEMENTS

Balance Sheet

Current Assets

Cash

Equity securities (investment of cash available for current operations)

Current debt securities available-for-sale

Accounts receivable

Inventories

Prepaid expenses

Current Liabilities

Short-term debt

Accounts payable

Accrued expenses

Current income taxes payable

Current portion of long-term debt

Unearned revenues

Balance Sheet (continued)

Long-Term Investments
Noncurrent debt securities available-for-sale
Noncurrent debt securities held-to-maturity
Investments at cost or equity

Property, Plant, and Equipment

Intangibles

Other Assets
Deposits
Deferred charges
Noncurrent deferred tax asset

Long-Term Debt
Long-term notes payable
Bonds payable
Noncurrent deferred tax liability

Stockholders' Equity
Preferred stock
Common stock
Additional paid-in capital
Retained earnings
Accumulated other comprehensive income

Current Assets and Liabilities

Assets
Economic resources
Future benefit
Control of company
Past event or transaction

Liabilities
Economic obligation
Future sacrifice
Beyond control of company
Past event or transaction

Current Assets
Converted into cash or used up

Longer of:
 One year
 One accounting cycle

Current Liabilities
Paid or settled
or Requires use of current assets
Longer of:
 One year
 One accounting cycle

Reporting the Results of Operations

Preparing an Income Statement

Multiple Steps	**Single Step**
Net Sales/Revenues	Net Sales/Revenues
− Cost of sales	+ Other income
= Gross profit	+ Gains
− Operating expenses	= Total revenues
Selling expenses	− Costs and expenses
General and administrative (G&A) expenses	Cost of sales
= Operating income	Selling expenses
+ Other income	G&A expenses
+ Gains	Other expenses
− Other expenses	Losses
− Losses	Income tax expense
= Income before taxes	= Income from continuing operations
− Income tax expense	
= Income from continuing operations	

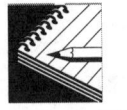

Reporting the Results of Operations (continued)

Computing Net Income

            Income from continuing operations (either approach)

±   Discontinued operations

=   Net income

(Cumulative changes section was eliminated by precodification SFAS 154.)

(Extraordinary item treatment was eliminated by ASU 2015-01.)

Unusual and Infrequently Occurring Items

Unusual nature exists when a transaction or event possesses a high degree of abnormality and is clearly unrelated, or incidental to, typical entity activities.

Infrequency of occurrence exists when the underlying transaction or event would not reasonably be expected to recur in the foreseeable future taking into account the entity's operating environment.

Items considered unusual, infrequently occurring, or both are to be reported as a separate item within income from continuing operations or disclosed in the notes to the financial statements.

1. Individually immaterial similar gains and losses shall be aggregated.
2. Items shall not be reported net of income tax and EPS impacts shall not be reported separately.

Reporting Comprehensive Income

Statement of comprehensive income required as one of the financial statements

- May be part of income statement
- May be separate statement
- Begin with net income
- Add or subtract items of other comprehensive income

Other comprehensive income includes (but is not limited to):

- Current year's unrealized gains or losses on available-for-sale debt securities
- Current year's foreign currency translation adjustments
- Current year's unrealized gains or losses (effective portion) on derivative instruments used as cash flow hedges

Reclassification Adjustments

- As unrealized gains (losses) recorded and reported in other comprehensive income for the current or prior periods are later realized, they are recognized and reported in net income. To avoid double counting, it is necessary to reverse unrealized amounts that have been recognized.

Statement of Changes in Equity

Statement provides beginning balances, changes during the year, and ending balances for the following items:

- Stock (common and preferred)
- Additional paid-in capital (APIC)
- Retained earnings
- Treasury stock
- Accumulated other comprehensive income (AOCI)

May be presented in footnotes, supplemental schedules, or as a separate statement

Statement of Cash Flows

Purpose of Statement

Summarizes sources and uses of cash, cash equivalents, and amounts generally described as restricted cash or restricted cash equivalents

Classifies cash flows into operating, investing, and financing activities

Cash Equivalents

Easily converted into cash (liquid)

Original maturity $\leq$ three months

Restrictions on Cash and Cash Equivalents

As a result of Accounting Standards Update No. 2016-18, *Statement of Cash Flows (Topic 230),* the statement of cash flows now presents the change during the period of cash, cash equivalents, and amounts generally described as restricted cash or restricted cash equivalents. Entities are also required to reconcile totals to amounts on the balance sheet and disclose the nature of the restrictions.

Format of Statement

Cash flows* provided or (used) by **operating** activities

±   Cash flows* provided or (used) by **investing** activities

±   Cash flows* provided or (used) by **financing** activities

=   Net increase or (decrease) in cash, cash equivalents, and restricted cash

+   Beginning balance

=   Ending balance

*Cash flows shall include cash, **cash equivalents,** and amounts generally described as restricted cash or restricted cash equivalents

Inputs to the Cash Flow Statement

The sources and uses of cash, cash equivalents, and restricted cash are categorized into operating, investing, and financing activities. In general:

Operating activities:

- Income statement items/adjustments (e.g., sales)
- Current assets and current liabilities (e.g., accounts receivable)

Investing activities:

- Noncurrent assets (e.g., building)

Financial activities:

- Noncurrent liabilities and equity (e.g., bank loan, stock)

Some changes do not involve cash, cash equivalents, or restricted cash (equipment purchased with stock), and some do not follow the general rule (e.g., dividends payable is a current liability, but since it is the result of stock ownership, its adjustment will appear in financing activities instead of operating activities).

Operating Activities

Direct Method: Top to bottom

Collections from customers
+ Interest and dividends received
+ Proceeds from sale of trading securities
+ Other operating inflows from cash, cash equivalents,
  or restricted cash
− Payments for merchandise
− Payments for expense
− Payments for interest
− Payments for income taxes
− Payments to acquire trading securities
− Other operating outflows from cash, cash equivalents,
  or restricted cash
= **Cash flows from operating activities**

Indirect Method: Top to bottom

Net income
Noncash revenues −
Noncash expenses +
Gains on sales of investments −
Losses on sales of investments +
Gains on sales of plant assets −
Losses on sales of plant assets +
Increases in current assets −
Decreases in current assets +
Decreases in current liabilities −
Increases in current liabilities +
Cash flows from operating activities =

Must be equal

Investing Activities

Principal collections on loans receivable

+ Proceeds from sale of investments (other than certain equity instruments carried in a trading account)

+ Proceeds from sale of plant assets

+ Proceeds from settlement of corporate-owned life insurance policies (premiums can be classified as either investing, operating, or a combination)

+ Some distributions received from equity method investees

− Loans made

− Payments to acquire investments (other than certain equity instruments carried in a trading account)

− Payments to acquire plant assets

− Payments made soon after acquisition date of a business combination to settle a contingent consideration liability

= **Cash flows from investing activities**

Financing Activities

Proceeds from borrowings

+   Proceeds from issuing stock

−   Debt principal payments, debt prepayment, or debt extinguishment costs

−   Payments to reacquire stock

−   Payments for dividends

−   Certain payments to settle a contingent consideration liability

=   **Cash flows from financing activities**

Components of Direct Method

Collections from customers (plug)	xxx	
Increase in accounts receivable (given)	xxx	
Decrease in accounts receivable (given)		xxx
Sales (given)		xxx
Increase in inventory (given)	xxx	
Decrease in accounts payable (given)	xxx	
Cost of sales (given)	xxx	
Decrease in inventory (given)		xxx
Increase in accounts payable (given)		xxx
Payments for merchandise (plug)		xxx

Adjustments under Indirect Method

- Credit changes are addbacks/debit changes are subtractions, for example:
  - Increase in accumulated depreciation added back
  - Increase in accounts payable added back
  - Increase in accounts receivable subtracted
  - Decrease in accounts payable subtracted
  - Decrease in accounts receivable added back

Other Disclosures

With direct method:

- Reconciliation of net income to cash flows from operating activities (indirect method)

With indirect method:

- Payments for interest
- Payments for income taxes

With all cash flow statements:

- Schedule of noncash investing and financing activities
- Information about nature of restrictions on cash, cash equivalents, and amounts generally described as restricted cash or restricted cash equivalents
- Line items and amounts of cash, cash equivalents, and amounts generally described as restricted cash or restricted cash equivalents reported within the statement of financial position (when presented in more than one line item within the statement of financial position)

IFRS and Cash Flows

- Interest/dividends in either financing or operations sections but must be consistent

Notes to Financial Statements

Basic Disclosures

Significant Accounting Policy Disclosures

- Inventory method
- Depreciation method
- Securities classified as cash and cash equivalents
- Basis for consolidation

Related Party Transactions

Liability disclosures

Capital structure

Errors and irregularities

Illegal acts

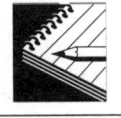

Risks and Uncertainties

- Nature of entity's operations
- Use of estimates in preparation of financial statements
- Certain significant estimates
- Current vulnerability due to significant concentrations
- Going-concern assessment

Subsequent Events

Events occurring after the balance sheet date but before the financial statements are issued or available to be issued. Measured through the issuance date.

Two types of events are possible:

1. Events that provide additional evidence about conditions existing at the balance sheet date (recognize in the financial statements)
2. Events that provide evidence about conditions that did not exist at the balance sheet date but arise subsequent to that date (disclose in the notes)

Subsequent Events (continued)

IFRS

- Subsequent events measured through date that the financial statements are authorized to be issued.
- IFRS does not require adjustment to balance sheet for share splits or reverse splits occurring after the reporting date but before the financial statements are issued.
- IFRS does not consider refinancing, amendments, or waivers when determining the classification of debt as current or noncurrent.

Evaluating Financial Statements

Ratios Involving Current Assets and Liabilities

Working capital = Current assets – Current liabilities

Current ratio = Current assets ÷ Current liabilities

Quick or Acid ratio = Quick assets ÷ Current liabilities

> Quick assets—current assets readily convertible into cash
> - Cash
> - Accounts receivable
> - Equity securities

Ratios Involving Receivables

Accounts receivable turnover = (Net) credit sales ÷ Average (net) accounts receivable

Days to collect accounts receivable = 365* ÷ Accounts receivable turnover

or

Days to collect accounts receivable = Average (net) accounts receivable ÷ Average (net) sales/day

Average (net) sales/day = (Net) credit sales ÷ 365*

*300 or 360 or 365 (or other measure of business days in a year)

Ratios Involving Inventories

Inventory turnover = Cost of goods sold ÷ Average inventory

Days sales in inventory = 365* ÷ Inventory turnover

or

Days sales in inventory = Average inventory ÷ Average inventory sold/day

Average inventory sold/day = Cost of sales ÷ 365*

*300 or 360 or 365 (or other measure of business days in a year)

Other Ratios

Debt to total assets = Total debt ÷ Total assets

Debt to equity = Total debt ÷ Total stockholders' equity

Return on assets = Net income ÷ Average total assets

Introduction to Consolidated Financial Statements

Objective is to present the financial statements as if it were one economic entity

Consolidation is required whenever one entity has effective control over another entity.

- Acquirer is the entity that obtains control of one or more businesses in the business combination
- Parent/investor ownership of majority of voting stock generally indicates control
- Control is also evident when an entity (variable-interest holder) is the principal beneficiary of a variable-interest entity
- Consolidation is not appropriate when a majority shareholder doesn't have effective control:
    - Company is in bankruptcy or reorganization
    - Foreign exchange controls limit power to keep control of subsidiary assets

Introduction to Consolidated Financial Statements (continued)

All consolidations are accounted for as acquisitions

- The acquirer shall recognize goodwill, the identifiable assets acquired, the liabilities assumed, and any noncontrolling interest in the acquiree
- Recognize separately
  - Acquisition-related costs
  - Assets acquired and liabilities assumed arising from *contractual contingencies*
  - Bargain purchase (fair value of assets acquired > amount paid) recognized as gain
  - Fair values of research and development assets
  - Changes in the value of acquirer deferred tax benefits

Parent's Accounting for a Subsidiary to be Consolidated

A Parent records a subsidiary on its books as an investment using:

- Cost method
- Equity method
- Any other method it chooses.

The method a Parent uses to carry an investment in a subsidiary on its books (cost, equity, or other) will not affect final resulting Consolidated Statements.

Accounting for an Acquisition

Combination—Records Combined

Assets (at fair market values)	xxx	
Separately identifiable assets	xxx	
Goodwill (plug)	xxx	
Liabilities (at fair market values)		xxx
Stockholders' equity (two steps)*		xxx
or		
Cash (amount paid)		xxx

* Credit common stock for par value of shares issued and credit additional paid-in capital (APIC) for difference between fair value and par value of shares issued.

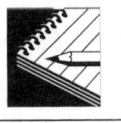

Consolidated Earnings—Year of Acquisition

Consolidated net income:

Parent's net income

+   Subsidiary's net income from date of acquisition

±   Effects of intercompany transactions

−   Depreciation on difference between fair value and carrying value of sub's assets

−   Impairment losses on goodwill (if applicable)

=   Consolidated net income

Retained Earnings—Year of Acquisition

Beginning retained earnings—Parent's beginning balance

+   Consolidated net income

−   Parent's dividends for entire period

=   Ending retained earnings

Consolidations

Eliminate the Investment

Example 1—Date of Combination—No Goodwill or Minority Interest

Inventory (excess of fair value over carrying value)	xxx	
Land (excess of fair value over carrying value)	xxx	
Depreciable assets (excess of fair value over carrying value)	xxx	
Common stock (sub's balance)	xxx	
Additional paid-in capital (APIC) (sub's balance)	xxx	
Retained earnings (sub's balance)	xxx	
Investment		xxx

Eliminate the Investment (continued)

Example 2 — Date of Combination — No Goodwill or Minority Interest

Inventory (excess of fair value over carrying value)	xxx	
Land (excess of fair value over carrying value)	xxx	
Depreciable assets (excess of fair value over carrying value)	xxx	
Common stock (sub's balance)	xxx	
APIC (sub's balance)	xxx	
Retained earnings (sub's balance)	xxx	
Minority interest (sub's total stockholders' equity × minority interest percentage)		xxx
Investment		xxx

Eliminate the Investment (continued)

Example 3—Date of Combination—Goodwill and Minority Interest

Inventory (excess of fair value over carrying value)	xxx
Land (excess of fair value over carrying value)	xxx
Depreciable assets (excess of fair value over carrying value)	xxx
Goodwill (plug)	**xxx**
Common stock (sub's balance)	xxx
APIC (sub's balance)	xxx
Retained earnings (sub's balance)	xxx

Minority interest (sub's total stockholders' equity × minority interest percentage)		xxx
Investment		xxx

Eliminate the Investment (continued)

Calculating Goodwill—Four Steps

1. Determine amount paid for acquisition
2. Compare to book value of sub's underlying net assets
3. Subtract difference between fair values and book values of sub's assets
4. Remainder is goodwill

Additional entries—After date of acquisition

- Debit cost of sales instead of inventory for fair market value (FMV) adjustment
- Recognize depreciation on excess of fair value over carrying value of depreciable assets
- Recognize impairment of goodwill (if FMV of goodwill is less than carrying amount)

Eliminating Entries

Intercompany Sales of Inventory

Eliminate gross amount of intercompany sales

Sales	xxx	
Cost of sales		xxx

Eliminate intercompany profit included in ending inventory

Cost of sales	xxx	
Inventory		xxx

Eliminate unpaid portion of intercompany sales

Accounts payable	xxx	
Accounts receivable		xxx

Eliminating Entries (continued)

Intercompany Sales of Property, Plant, and Equipment

Eliminate intercompany gain or loss

Gain on sale (amount recognized)	xxx	
Depreciable asset		xxx

Adjust depreciation

Accumulated depreciation (amount of gain divided by remaining useful life)	xxx	
Depreciation expense		xxx

Eliminating Entries (continued)

Intercompany Bond Holdings

Eliminate intercompany investment in bonds

Bonds payable (face amount of bonds acquired)	xxx		
Bond premium or discount (amount related to intercompany bonds)	xxx	or	xxx
Gain or loss on retirement (plug)	xxx	or	xxx
Investment in bonds (carrying value)			xxx

Variable Interest Entities (VIEs)

Previously known as special-purpose entities

Control is achieved based on contractual, ownership, or other pecuniary interests.

Primary beneficiary—The entity that has controlling financial interest in the VIE and must consolidate it. This must be reassessed every year.

Both conditions must exist for control:

1. Having the power to direct the significant activities of the VIE
2. The entity has the obligation to absorb significant losses of the VIE or the right to receive significant benefits

Qualitative approach used to determine control when power is shared among unrelated parties, which could lead to none of the entities consolidating the VIE.

Kick-out rights—The ability to remove the reporting entity who has the power to direct the VIE's significant activities.

Variable Interest Entities (VIEs) (*continued*)

Participating rights—The ability to block the reporting entity with the power to direct the VIE's significant activities.

Protective rights—rights that protect the party holding the rights but do not give that party controlling financial interests.

Discontinued Operations

A discontinued operation occurs when a component or group of components of an entity are 1) disposed for by sale or other than sale, or classified as held-for-sale, and 2) the disposal "represents a strategic shift that has (or will have) a major effect on an entity's operation and financial results." (ASU 2014-08) A "strategic shift" includes the disposal of a major geographical area, a major line of business, a major equity method investment, or other major parts of the entity.

The income of a discontinued operation, and any gain or loss from its disposal, are separated from income from continuing operations, for all periods presented, even though in previous periods the income from the segment was part of continuing operations.

Reporting Discontinued Operations

Income statement: Discontinued operations are reported below income from continuing operations

- Income—Income from the discontinued operation (DOP) for the portion of the year to disposal (or if disposal occurs in a later year, income for the entire year).

- Gain or loss—On disposal of the operation. The gain or loss is the net proceeds from sale of the component less book value of the component's net assets. Net proceeds are equal to the gross amount received on sale less the cost to dispose of the assets.

Actual gains on disposal (when the decision to discontinue the operation and the disposal occur in the same period) are recognized but estimated gains are not.

If the book value of the net assets of the component exceeds the component's fair value less cost of disposal at year-end, then the component assets are written down to fair value less cost of disposal (loss is recognized even if disposal or sale has not taken place).

- All items reported for discontinued operations are net of tax (after tax).

- Earnings per share is presented for discontinued operations on the face of the income statement.

Balance sheet

- All assets and liabilities of the discontinued operation for all comparative periods are presented separately on the balance sheet.

Reporting Discontinued Operations (continued)

Additional disclosures:

- Major classes of line items comprising the discontinued operation
- Either (a) total operating and investing cash flows or (b) depreciation
- Amortization, capital expenditures, and significant operating and investing noncash items
- Applicable non-controlling interest profit/loss
- Asset/liability reconciliation between notes and statements
- Profit/loss reconciliation between notes and statements
- Disposals that do not qualify for discontinued operations
- Significant involvement with discontinued operations
- Facts and circumstances leading to the disposal

PUBLIC COMPANY REPORTING TOPICS (SEC, EPS, INTERIM, AND SEGMENT)

SEC Reporting Requirements

Regulation S-X describes form and content to be filed

Regulation S-K describes information requirements

- Form S-1 (US)/F-1 (foreign)—Registration statement
- Form 8-K (US)/6-K (foreign)—Material event
- Form 10-K (US)/20F (foreign)—Annual report
- Form 10Q—Quarterly report
- Schedule 14A—Proxy statement

Regulation AB describes asset-backed securities reporting

Regulation Fair Disclosure (FD) mandates material information disclosures

- Compliance through an 8-K issuance

Earnings per Share (EPS)

Reporting Earnings per Share

Simple capital structure

- No potentially dilutive securities outstanding
- Present basic EPS only

Complex capital structure

- Potentially dilutive securities outstanding
- Dual presentation of EPS—basic EPS and diluted EPS

Potentially dilutive securities—Securities that can be converted into common shares

- Convertible bonds and convertible preferred stock
- Options, rights, and warrants

Basic EPS

Numerator

Income available to common stockholders

Income from continuing operations
- − Dividends declared on noncumulative preferred stock
- − Current dividends on cumulative preferred stock (whether or not declared)
- = Income from continuing operations available to common stockholders
- ± Discontinued operations
- = Net income available to common stockholders

Denominator

Weighted-average common shares outstanding on the balance sheet date

Diluted EPS

Adjust numerator and denominator for dilutive securities

- Assume conversion into common shares
- Dilutive if EPS decreases

Convertible Preferred Stock

Dilutive if basic EPS is greater than preferred dividend per share of common stock obtainable:

- Add preferred dividends back to numerator
- Add common shares that preferred would be converted into to denominator

Convertible Bonds

Dilutive if basic EPS is greater than interest, net of tax, per share of common stock obtainable

- Add interest, net of tax, to numerator
- Add common shares that bonds would be converted into to denominator

Options, Rights, and Warrants

Dilutive when market price exceeds exercise price (proceeds from exercise)

The **treasury stock method** is applied

    Number of options ⟶ Number of options
    ×   Exercise price
    =   Proceeds from exercise
    ÷   Average market price of stock during period
    =   Shares reacquired with proceeds ⟶ − Shares reacquired
                                       =   Increase in denominator

Calculation done on quarter-by-quarter basis

Presentation of EPS Information

Income Statement

Simple capital structure—Basic EPS only

- Income from continuing operations
- Net income

Complex capital structure—Basic and diluted EPS

- Income from continuing operations
- Net income

Additional Disclosures (Income Statement or Notes)

- Discontinued operations

Segment Reporting

Definition of Segments

Operating segments identified using management approach:

- Component earns revenue and incurs expenses
- Separate information is available
- Component is evaluated regularly by top management

Not all subunits are operating segments.

Reportable Segments—Three Tests

1. Revenue test—Segment revenues ≥ 10% of total revenues

2. Asset test—Segment identifiable assets ≥ 10% of total assets

3. Profit or loss test (absolute value)

   - Combine profits (pretax) for all profitable segments
   - Combine losses for all losing segments
   - Select larger amount
   - Segments profit or loss ≥ 10% of larger amount

Disclosures for Reportable Segments

Factors used to identify operating segments

General information about products and services of operating segment

Segment profit or loss

- Segment revenues include intersegment sales
- Deduct traceable operating expenses and allocated indirect operating expenses
- Do not deduct general corporate expenses

Segment revenues

Segment assets

Interest revenue and expense

Depreciation, depletion, and amortization

Other items

Interim Reporting

General Rules

1. Revenues and expenses recognized in interim period when performance obligation is met or incurred
2. Same principles as applied to annual financial statements

Interim Reporting—Special Rules

Inventory Losses

Expected to recover within annual period—Temporary declines

- Not recognized in interim period
- Later recoveries not recorded because the previous loss was not recorded

Not expected to recover within annual period—Permanent declines

- Recognized in interim period
- Recoveries recognized as gains to the extent of previous losses only
- Inventory may not be marked up above cost

Income Taxes

Estimate of rate that applies to annual period

Interim Reporting—Other Items

Property taxes—Allocated among interim periods

Repairs and maintenance

- Generally recognized in interim period when incurred (including major repairs)
- Allocated to current and subsequent interim periods when future benefit results

Disposal of a segment—Recognized in interim period in which it occurs

Interim Reporting—IFRS

- Discrete report, therefore use same accounting policies as in year-end financial statements
- Not required

SPECIAL PURPOSE FRAMEWORKS

Private Company Council (PCC)

The Private Company Council (PCC) is an organization that assists in setting accounting standards for private companies.

Private company—"an entity other than a **public business entity**, a **not-for-profit entity**, or an employee benefit plan within the scope of Topics 960 through 965 on plan accounting."

The PCC has two principal responsibilities:

- Work with (FASB) to identify opportunities for alternative accounting for private companies within (GAAP)
- Serve in an advisory capacity to the FASB on appropriate treatment of items under consideration for new GAAP and how those items may impact private companies.

Private Company Council (PCC) (continued)

Significant differential factors between public business entities (public companies) and private companies:

- Number of primary users and their access to management
- Investment strategies of primary users
- Ownership and capital structure
- Accounting resources
- Learning about new financial reporting guidance

Examines the following for differential guidance:

- Recognition and measurement
- Disclosures
- Display
- Effective date
- Transition method

Private Company Council (PCC) (continued)

Adoption and Transition to PCC Standards

- Private companies can elect to adopt PCC alternatives at the beginning of any annual period with no retrospective application
- Adoption of PCC alternative without assessing the preferability of the PCC alternative

CASH AND CASH EQUIVALENTS

Bank Reconciliation

Bank balance
+ Deposits in transit
− Outstanding checks
± Errors made by bank
= Corrected balance

Book balance
Amounts collected by bank +
Unrecorded bank charges −
Errors made when recording transactions ±
Corrected balance =

Must be equal

ACCOUNTS RECEIVABLE—ACCOUNTING AND REPORTING

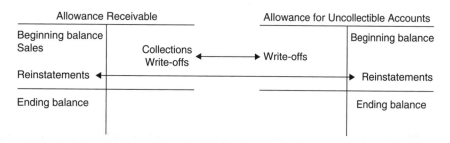

Recorded at net realizable value = Accounts receivable – Allowance for uncollectible accounts

Recording Methods

1. Gross method—Records receivables at gross invoice price (before cash discount)
2. Net method—Records receivables at net invoice price (after cash discount)

Uncollectible Accounts—Direct Write-Off and Allowance

Allowance Methods—GAAP

Matching concept—Bad debt expense in period of sale

Measurement concept—Accounts receivable at net realizable value

Direct Write-off Method—Non-GAAP

Violates matching concept—Bad debt expense when account written off

Violates measurement concept—Accounts receivable overstated at gross amount

Allowance Account—Income Statement and Balance Sheet Approach

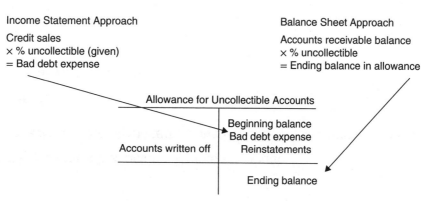

Income Statement Approach

Credit sales
× % uncollectible (given)
= Bad debt expense

Balance Sheet Approach

Accounts receivable balance
× % uncollectible
= Ending balance in allowance

Allowance for Uncollectible Accounts

	Beginning balance
	Bad debt expense
Accounts written off	Reinstatements
	Ending balance

Calculate expense and plug balance **or** calculate balance and plug expense.

Notes Receivable

- Recorded at the present value of future cash flows (long term)
- Discount rate used is market rate of interest on date of note creation

Notes Received for Cash

PV of future cash flows = Cash that exchanged hands on the date of note creation

Calculating Payment

Principal amount ÷ Present value factor = Payment amount

    Present value factor for annuity based on number of payments and interest rate

Allocating Payments

Payment amount − Interest = Principal reduction

Calculating Interest

Beginning balance
  × Interest rate
  × Period up to payment
  = Interest up to payment

Balance after principal reduction
  × Interest rate
  × Period up to payment to year-end
  = Interest for remainder of year

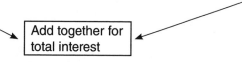

Add together for
total interest

Notes Received for Goods or Services

Note Balance

Short term: Amount = Face value

Long term: Amount = Fair value of goods or services

Present value of future cash flows if more clearly determined or if fair value not known

Journal entry:

Note receivable—Face amount (given)	xxx	
Revenue—Calculated amount		xxx
Discount on note receivable (plug)		xxx

Notes Received for Goods or Services (continued)

Interest Income

Face amount of note

−   Unamortized discount

=   Carrying value of note

×   Interest rate

=   Interest income

Journal Entry:

Discount on note receivable	xxx	
Interest income		xxx

Discounting Receivables

Proceeds from Discounting

Face amount

+ Interest income (Face × Interest rate × Term)

= Maturity value

− Discount (Maturity value × Discount rate × Remaining term)

= Proceeds

Factoring

Factoring without Recourse

Treated as a sale

Cash (Accounts receivable balance less fee less holdback)	xxx	
Due from factor (holdback)*	xxx	
Loss on sale (fee charged by the factor)	xxx	
Accounts receivable (balance)		xxx

* Due from factor (receivable) is an amount the factor holds back in case customers return merchandise to the business selling the receivables. If customers return the merchandise, they will not be paying the factor.

Factoring with Recourse

Can either be treated as a sale or loan

Treated as Sale

Cash (Accounts receivable balance less fee less holdback)	xxx	
Due from factor (holdback)	xxx	
Loss on sale (fee charged by the factor + recourse value)	xxx	
Accounts receivable (balance)		xxx
Recourse liability*		xxx

* The recourse liability is assigned a fair value and initially increases the loss.
If receivables are 100% collected by the factor, the recourse will be reversed:

Recourse liability	xxx	
Loss on sale		xxx

*When accounts are deemed uncollectible, the transferor remits the necessary cash to the factor:

Recourse liability	xxx	
Cash		xxx

Assignment of Receivables

Treated as Loan

Cash—Proceeds (given)	xxx	
Note payable secured by receivables		xxx
Accounts receivable assigned	xxx	
Accounts receivable (balance)		xxx

INVENTORY

Ending Inventory

Merchandise owned by a business enterprise on the last day of the accounting year, regardless of location, is included in ending inventory

Goods in Transit—Ownership Determined by Legal Title

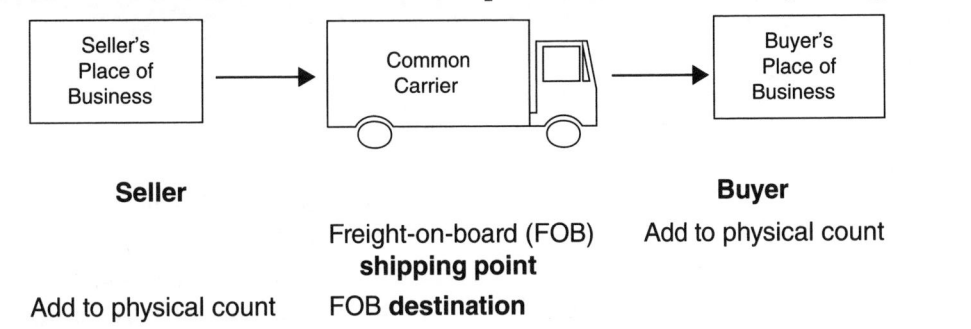

Seller		Buyer
		Add to physical count
	Freight-on-board (FOB) **shipping point**	
Add to physical count	FOB **destination**	

Ending Inventory (continued)

Goods on Consignment need to be considered for ending inventory
Consignee—Exclude from physical count
Consignor—Add to physical count (at cost)

Valuation of Inventory
Purchase price

+ Freight in

+ Costs incurred in preparing for sale
    (such as insurance in transit, taxes,
    handling costs, packaging costs, etc)

= Inventory cost

Cost of goods on consignment =
Inventory cost
+ Cost of shipping to consignee

Selling, general, and administrative expenditures as well as abnormal costs are expensed in current period instead of being included in inventory abnormal costs include:

- Idle facility expense
- Wasted materials in production and excess spoilage
- Double freight when items returned and redelivered

Periodic versus Perpetual Inventory System and Cost Flow Assumption

	Periodic	Perpetual

Buy merchandise	Purchases
	    Accounts payable
		Inventory
		    Accounts payable

Sell merchandise	Accounts receivable
	    Sales
		Accounts receivable
		    Sales
		COGS sold (COGS)
		    Inventory

Record COGS	Ending inventory (count)
	COGS (plug)
	    Purchases (net amount)
	    Beginning inventory (balance)	

First in, first out (FIFO)—Same under either method

Last in, first out (LIFO)—Different amounts for periodic and perpetual

Average—Different amounts for periodic and perpetual

    Periodic—Weighted average

Focus on
Inventory

94

Cost of Goods Sold (COGS)—Periodic System

To calculate cost of goods sold for a company employing the periodic inventory system, the calculation shown below is used.

Beginning inventory

+   Net purchases

=   Cost of goods available for sale

−   Ending inventory

=   Cost of goods sold (COGS)

Evaluation of FIFO and LIFO

	Ending Inventory	Cost of Goods Sold	Gross Profit
Periods of rising prices:			
FIFO	Highest	Lowest	Highest
LIFO	Lowest	Highest	Lowest
Periods of falling prices:			
FIFO	Lowest	Highest	Lowest
LIFO	Highest	Lowest	Highest

FIFO Application—Valuing Cost Of Sales and Ending Inventory

The earliest purchased goods are assumed to be sold first

Cost of sales and ending inventory values are identical under perpetual and periodic methods

Example: Beginning inventory = 0; Ending Inventory = 15,000

	Purchases	Price per unit	Total cost
January	10,000 units	$5.00	$50,000
April	12,000 units	$5.50	$66,000
July	15,000 units	$6.00	$90,000
November	13,500 units	$6.50	$87,750
Total	55,000 units		$293,750

Calculate the value of ending inventory and cost of sales:

Ending inventory = 15,000 units (given) = November 13,500 units × $6.50 + July 1,500 units × $6.00 = $96,750 (ending inventory consists of the latest purchased units).

Cost of sales: Total available − Ending inventory = $293,750 − 96,750 = $197,000

LIFO Application—Valuing Cost of Sales and Ending Inventory Using the Periodic Method

The earliest purchased goods are assumed to be sold last

Cost of sales and ending inventory values are different under perpetual and periodic methods

Example of periodic method: Beginning inventory = 0; Ending Inventory = 15,000

	Purchases	Price per unit	Total cost
January	10,000 units	$5.00	$50,000
April	12,000 units	$5.50	$66,000
July	15,000 units	$6.00	$90,000
November	13,500 units	$6.50	$87,750
Total	55,000 units		$293,750

Calculate the value of ending inventory and cost of sales:

Ending inventory = 15,000 units (given) = January 10,000 units × $5.00 + April 5,000 units × $5.50 = $77,500 (ending inventory consists of earliest purchased units)

Cost of sales: Total available − Ending inventory = $293,750 − 77,500 = $216,250

Applying LIFO Layers

Step 1. Determine ending quantity.

Step 2. Compare to previous period's ending quantity.

Step 3. Increases—Add new layer.

Step 4. Small decreases (less than most recent layer)—Reduce most recent layer.

Step 5. Large decreases (more than most recent layer)—Eliminate most recent layer or layers and decrease next most recent layer.

Step 6. Apply appropriate unit price to each layer.

For each layer:

$$\text{Inventory quantity} \times \text{Price per unit} = \text{Inventory value}$$

Application of LIFO Layers

Information Given:

	Ending Quantity	Price per unit
Year 1	10,000 units	$5.00
Year 2	12,000 units	$5.50
Year 3	15,000 units	$6.00
Year 4	13,500 units	$6.50
Year 5	11,200 units	$7.00
Year 6	13,200 units	$7.50

Information Applied:

Year 1:

Base layer	10,000 units		$5.00	$50,000
Total	**10,000 units**			**$50,000**

Application of LIFO Layers (continued)

Year 2:

Year 2 layer	2,000 units	$5.50	$11,000
Base layer	10,000 units	$5.00	$50,000
Total	**12,000 units**		**$61,000**

Year 3:

Year 3 layer	3,000 units	$6.00	$18,000
Year 2 layer	2,000 units	$5.50	$11,000
Base layer	10,000 units	$5.00	$50,000
Total	**15,000 units**		**$79,000**

Application of LIFO Layers (continued)

Year 4:

Year 3 layer	1,500 units	$6.00	$9,000
Year 2 layer	2,000 units	$5.50	$11,000
Base layer	10,000 units	$5.00	$50,000
Total	**13,500 units**		**$70,000**

Year 5:

Year 2 layer	1,200 units	$5.50	$6,600
Base layer	10,000 units	$5.00	$50,000
Total	**11,200 units**		**$56,600**

Application of LIFO Layers (continued)

Year 6:

Year 3 layer	2,000 units	$7.50	$15,000
Year 2 layer	1,200 units	$5.50	$6,600
Base layer	10,000 units	$5.00	$50,000
Total	**13,200 units**		**$71,600**

Dollar-Value LIFO

- Reduces effect of LIFO liquidation
- Allows companies to use FIFO internally
- Reduces clerical costs
- Combines inventory into pools
- Uses conversion index

  Conversion Index = Ending inventory in CY Dollars/Ending Inventory in base-year dollars

- Objective is to convert FIFO ending inventory to LIFO for Financial Statement reporting purposes

Applying Dollar-Value LIFO

Step 1. Determine ending inventory at current year's costs

Step 2. Divide by current price level index to convert to base-year costs

Step 3. Compare to previous period's ending inventory at base-year costs to determine quantity change.

Step 4. Increases—Add new layer at base-year costs

Step 5. Small decreases (less than most recent layer)—Reduce most recent layer

Step 6. Large decreases (more than most recent layer)—Eliminate most recent layer or layers and decrease next most recent layer

Step 7. Convert current-year layer to current-year costs

For each layer:

$$\text{Inventory amount at base-year costs} \times \text{Price index} = \text{Inventory amount dollar-value LIFO}$$

Application of Dollar Value LIFO

Information given:

	Ending Inventory at Current Costs	Price Level Index
Year 1	$200,000	100
Year 2	243,800	106
Year 3	275,000	110
Year 4	255,200	116

Information applied:

Year 1

		Base-Year Costs	Index	Dollar-Value LIFO
Base layer		$200,000	100	$200,000
	Total	$200,000		$200,000

Application of Dollar Value LIFO (continued)

Year 2:

$243,800 ÷ 1.06 = $230,000 (at base-year costs)

	Base-Year Costs	Index	Dollar-Value LIFO
Year 2 layer	$30,000	106	$31,800
Base layer	$200,000	100	$200,000
Total	$230,000		$231,800

Application of Dollar Value LIFO (continued)

Year 3:

$275,000 ÷ 1.10 = $250,000 (at base-year costs)

	Base-Year Costs	Index	Dollar-Value LIFO
Year 3 layer	$20,000	110	$22,000
Year 2 layer	$30,000	106	$31,800
Base layer	$200,000	100	$200,000
Total	$250,000		$253,800

Application of Dollar-Value LIFO (continued)

Year 4:

$255,200 ÷ 1.16 = $220,000 (at base-year costs)

	Base-Year Costs	Index	Dollar-Value LIFO
Year 2 layer	$20,000	106	$21,200
Base layer	$200,000	100	$200,000
Total	$220,000		$221,200

Dollar-Value LIFO—Calculating a Price Level Index

Simplified LIFO—Company uses a published index

Double Extension Method—Cumulative index

Compare current year to base year

$$\frac{\text{Ending inventory at current year's costs}}{\text{Ending inventory at base-year costs}}$$

Link Chain Method—Annual index

Compare current year to previous year

$$\frac{\text{Ending inventory at current year's costs}}{\text{Ending inventory at previous year's costs}}$$

Lower of Cost or Net Realizable Value

Lower of cost or net realizable value replaces subsequent measurement for all inventory methods except LIFO and the retail inventory method (for which lower of cost or market still applies).

- Subsequent valuation of inventories carried at FIFO or weighted average are measured at the lower of the cost basis or net realizable value.
- Net realizable value is the "estimated selling prices in the ordinary course of business, less reasonably predictable cost of completion, disposal, and transportation." (FASB Accounting Standards Codification Master Glossary)

Lower of Cost or Market*

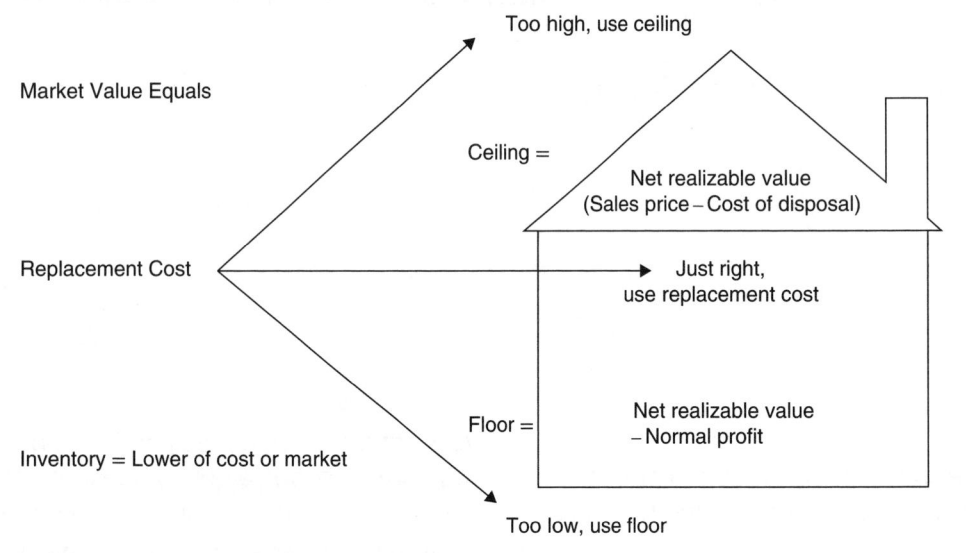

Market Value Equals

Too high, use ceiling

Ceiling =

Net realizable value
(Sales price – Cost of disposal)

Replacement Cost

Just right,
use replacement cost

Floor =

Net realizable value
– Normal profit

Inventory = Lower of cost or market

Too low, use floor

*Used for LIFO and Retail Inventory Method only

Gross Margin Method for Estimating Inventory*

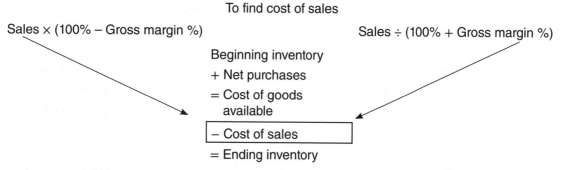

If gross margin is percentage of sales:

= Gross profit/Sales

If gross margin is percentage of cost:

= Gross profit/Cost of sales

To find cost of sales

Sales × (100% − Gross margin %)

Sales ÷ (100% + Gross margin %)

Beginning inventory

+ Net purchases

= Cost of goods available

− Cost of sales

= Ending inventory

*The gross margin method can be used only for estimation purposes. It may not be used for financial reporting of inventory."

Conventional Retail (Lower of Cost or Market)*

	Cost	Retail	C/R%
Beginning inventory	xx	xx	
+ Net purchases	xx	xx	
+ Freight in	<u>xx</u>		
+ Net markups		<u>xx</u>	
= Cost of goods available for sale	xx	xx	Cost/Retail
– Sales (retail)	xx		
Net markdowns	xx		
Employee discounts	xx		
Spoilage (retail)	xx	(<u>xx</u>)	
= Ending inventory at retail		xx	
x Cost to retail percentage		x%	
= Ending inventory at approximate lower of cost or market		<u>xx</u>	

*Variation of Retail Inventory Method also referred to as Average, Lower of Cost or Market

Focus on
Inventory

Inventory Errors

	Beg. Retained Earnings	COGS	Gross Profit	End Retained Earnings
Beginning—overstated	Over	Over	Under	No effect
Beginning—understated	Under	Under	Over	No effect
Ending—overstated	No effect	Under	Over	Over
Ending—understated	No effect	Over	Under	Under

Inventory and IFRS

- LIFO not permissible
- Lower of cost or net realizable value (LCNRV) on item-by-item basis
- Same cost formulas must be used for inventory with a similar nature and use
- Reversal of write down to net realizable value permitted
- Cost flow assumption mirrors physical flow

PROPERTY, PLANT, AND EQUIPMENT

Capitalized Costs

Capitalized amount = Cash Equivalent or Negotiated Acquisition Cost + Costs incurred in preparing it for its intended use (get-ready costs)

Get ready costs include:

    Shipping
    Insurance during shipping
    Installation
    Testing

Valuation

Cash equivalent price or negotiated acquisition cost

- Cash purchase—Cash paid
- Deferred payment plan (credit purchase)—Present value of future cash payments using market rate of interests for similar debt instruments
- Issuance of securities—Fair value of the security or the fair value of the asset acquired, whichever can be most clearly determined
- Donated assets—Recorded at fair value; a revenue or gain is also recorded
- Group purchases—Allocated based on the respective fair values of the individual assets acquired

Group Purchases—Application

Land and building—total cost:

- Purchase price
- Delinquent taxes assumed
- Legal fees
- Title insurance

Allocation to land and building:

$$\begin{array}{l} \text{FV of land} \\ \underline{+ \text{ FV of building}} \\ = \text{Total FV} \end{array}$$

Land = (FV of land ÷ Total FV) × Total cost

Building = (FV of building ÷ Total FV) × Total cost

Focus on
Property, Plant, and Equipment

Interest Capitalization Basics

Capitalize on:

- Significant plant assets constructed for sale or lease, or for company's own use

Do not capitalize on inventory manufactured in the ordinary course of business

Interest capitalized:

- Lesser of actual interest cost incurred during construction period or avoidable interest
- Avoidable interest = Interest rate × Average accumulated expenditures (AAE)

Interest on other debt that could be avoided by repayment of debt

Interest rate to use:

- Weighted-average method
- Specific interest method

Post-Acquisition Expenditures

Capitalize if:

- **Additions**—The cost makes the asset bigger, such as an addition to a building
- **Modifications/improvements**—The cost makes the asset better, such as an improvement that makes an asset perform more efficiently
- **Extends the useful life**—The cost makes the asset last longer.

Do not capitalize:

Repairs and maintenance

Depreciation and Depletion

Basic Terms:

Straight-line rate = 100% ÷ Useful life (in years)

Book value = Cost – Accumulated depreciation

Depreciable basis = Cost – Salvage value

Selection of Method:

Use **straight-line** when benefit from asset is uniform over life

Use **accelerated** when:

- Asset more productive in earlier years
- Costs of maintenance increase in later years
- Risk of obsolescence is high

Use **units-of-production** when usefulness decreases with use

Depreciation Methods

Straight-Line

Annual depreciation =
Depreciable basis
× Straight-line rate

Partial year =
Annual depreciation
× Portion of year

Double-Declining Balance

Annual depreciation =
Book value
× Straight-line rate
× 2

Partial year =
Book value
× Straight-line rate
× 2
× Portion of year

Service hours Method

Depreciation Rate = (Cost − Salvage value) / Useful life in service hours
Depreciation = Depreciation rate × Service hours for year

Property, Plant, and Equipment

Depreciation Methods (continued)

Sum-of-the-Years' Digits

Annual depreciation = **Depreciable basis** × Fraction

	1st Year	2nd Year	3rd Year
Numerator =	n	$n - 1$	$n - 2$
Denominator =	$n(n + 1) \div 2$	$n(n + 1) \div 2$	$n(n + 1) \div 2$

Partial year:

1st year =	1st year's depreciation × Portion of year
2nd year =	Remainder of 1st year's depreciation + 2nd year's depreciation × Portion of year
3rd year =	Remainder of 2nd year's depreciation + 3rd year's depreciation × Portion of year

Depreciation methods (continued)

Units of Production

Depreciation rate = **Depreciable basis** ÷ Total estimated units to be produced (hours)

Annual depreciation = Depreciation rate × Number of units produced (hours used)

Group or Composite

Applies straight-line method to groups of assets rather than to assets individually

Gains or losses not recognized on disposal

Cash (proceeds)	xx	
Accumulated depreciation (plug)	xx	
Asset (original cost)		xx

Impairment—Assets for Use and Held-for-Sale

Indications of impairment:

- Significant decrease in the market value of the asset
- Significant change in the way asset is used or physical change in asset
- An adverse action or assessment by a regulator
- An operating or cash flow loss associated with a revenue producing asset
- Asset is sold before the end of its expected life

Impairment—assets held-for-use:

- An asset for use is impaired if carrying value (CV) > undiscounted cash flows (UCF)
- Asset is written down to fair value (or discounted net cash flow):

Loss due to impairment (BV less FV)	xx	
Accumulated depreciation		xx

- Depreciate new basis
- No reversal of loss

Note that test for impairment (future cash flow) is different from impairment loss (CV − FV).

Impairment—Assets for Use and Held-for-Sale (continued)

An impairment loss occurs for an asset held-for-sale when CV > FV less cost to sell:

- Asset is written down to fair value less cost to sell
- No depreciation
- Reversal permitted

Application of Impairment Rules—Asset for Use

Example 1:

    Asset carrying value: $1,000,000

    Undiscounted future cash flow expected from asset: $900,000

    Fair market value of asset: $600,000

    Impairment exists: $900,000 expected cash flow less than $1,000,000 carrying amount

    Write asset down by $400,000 ($1,000,000 reduced to $600,000)

Example 2:

    Asset carrying value: $800,000

    Undiscounted future cash flow expected from asset: $900,000

    Fair market value of asset: $600,000

    No impairment adjustment: $900,000 expected cash flow exceeds $800,000 carrying amount

Disposal of Property, Plant, and Equipment

Cash (proceeds)	xx
Accumulated depreciation (balance)	xx
Loss on disposal (plug)	xx
Gain on disposal (plug)	xx
Asset (original cost)	xx

A disposal in **involuntary conversion** is recorded in the same manner as a sale.

Impairment and IFRS

- Impairment of long-lived assets is tested annually at the individual asset level, where possible.
- Impairment loss exists if the carrying amount of the asset exceeds the recoverable amount of the asset.
- IFRS uses a one-step process. Impairment loss = Carrying amount – Recoverable amount
- Recoverable amount is greater of:

    1. Fair value – Costs to sell or
    2. Present value of future cash flows to be derived from asset

- Impairment losses can be reversed if circumstances change (except for goodwill)

PPE and IFRS

- Estimated useful life and depreciation method reviewed annually
- Component depreciation required in some cases
- PPE can be revalued to fair value
- Interest earned on construction funds can offset the interest costs

NONMONETARY EXCHANGES

- Involve nonmonetary assets
- Either have commercial substance or no commercial substance

Nonmonetary Exchanges with Commercial Substance

- Cash flows from new asset are significantly different from those of old asset (amount, timing, risk,) or
- Use of new asset is significantly different from old asset
- Record a gain or loss based on difference in the outgoing asset's FV and BV
- Value the incoming asset at FV

Cash (amount received)		
Asset—New (FV)	xx	
Accumulated depreciation (balance on old asset)	xx	
Loss on revaluation of old asset (plug)		
Cash (amount paid)		
Gain on disposal (plug)		xx
Asset—Old (Original cost)		xx

Nonmonetary Exchanges with Commercial Substance (continued)

If FV not determinable: recognize no gain or loss

Record acquired asset as follows:

BV of asset given

\+   Cash paid

–   Cash received

Nonmonetary Exchanges with No Commercial Substance

- Cash flows from acquired asset will not be significantly different from asset exchanged (amount, timing, or risk); or
- Use value of acquired asset is not significantly different, in relation to the FV of the assets exchanged
- Incoming (new) asset is recorded at the BV of the asset given

Exception to BV reporting when there is no commercial substance:

- If a loss is evident, it is recognized in full, and the acquired asset is recorded at market value. Cash can be paid or received on the exchange for this exception
- If a gain is evident and cash is received (only), gain is recognized in proportion to the amount of cash received, and acquired asset is recorded at market value less portion of gain unrecognized. Entire gain will be recognized if proportion represented by cash is 25% or more, and acquired asset is recorded at fair value.

Nonmonetary Exchanges with No Commercial Substance (continued)

Loss—FV of asset given < Carrying value of asset given

Cash (amount received)	xx	
Asset—New (FV)	xx	
Loss on disposal (plug)	xx	
Cash (amount paid)		xx
Asset—Old (carrying value)		xx

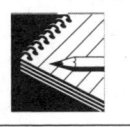

Nonmonetary Exchanges with No Commercial Substance (continued)

Gain—FV of asset given > Carrying value of asset given

Gain recognized only when cash received

FV of asset given
  − Carrying value of asset given
  = Total gain
  × Percentage
  = Gain recognized

$$\frac{\text{Cash received}}{\text{Total proceeds (Cash + FV of asset received)}}$$

Cash (amount received)	xx	
Asset—New (plug)	xx	
Gain on disposal (computed amount)		xx
Asset—Old (carrying value)		xx

Nonmonetary Exchanges with No Commercial Substance (continued)

No gain recognized when cash paid or no cash involved

Asset—New (plug)	xx	
Accumulated depreciation (balance on old asset)	xx	
Cash (amount paid)		xx
Asset—Old (original cost)		xx

INVESTMENTS

Equity Securities

- Include common stock, preferred stock (except redeemable preferred stock), stock warrants, call options/rights, put options
- Exclude debt securities (including convertible debt), redeemable preferred stock, and treasury stock

Debt Securities

- Include bonds, notes, convertible bonds/notes, redeemable preferred stock
- Exclude common/preferred stock, stock warrants/options/rights, futures/forward contracts

Note: ASU 2016-01, *Financial Instruments—Overall: Recognition and Measurement of Financial Assets and Financial Liabilities* significantly changed the accounting for investments in the equity of another entity. This standard is effective for fiscal years beginning after December 15, 2017, and is eligible for testing on the CPA Exam beginning January 1, 2018

Valuation and Reporting of Equity Investments

Percentage Equity Ownership	<20%	≥20%–50%	>50%
Level of economic influence	Nominal	Significant	Control
Valuation basis	If readily determinable FV, use FV. If not, cost less impairment.	Equity method unless FV option is elected.	Equity method or cost method
Balance sheet presentation	As investment: current or noncurrent based on intent to hold	As investment: typical noncurrent	Consolidated financial statements

Accounting for Equity Investments at Fair Value

- Equity investments are carried at FV (unless certain exceptions are met)
- Initial recognition is price paid, and includes purchase price plus costs directly related to purchase (brokerage fees, transfer fees, etc.)
- Dividends received are recognized as income in period earned
- Subsequent measurement of equity investment is at FV excluding transaction costs
- Unrealized gains or losses reported in earnings

Cost Method–Equity Securities

When there is no readily determinable fair value, the investor may elect the practicability exception to carry the investment at cost:

- Election of the practicability exception applies only to equity investments that do not qualify for using net asset value (NAV) as the practical expedient for fair value
- Initial purchase of equity security recorded at cost
- Dividend income recorded in net income
- Impairment losses recorded against the investment in the equity security carried at cost

Equity Method

Carrying Value of Investment

Cost

+   Earnings

−   Dividends

=   Carrying value of investment

Earnings

Income reported by investee

×   % of ownership

=   Unadjusted amount

−   Adjustments

=   Investor's share of investee's earnings

Equity Method—Adjustments to Earnings

1. Compare initial investment to FV of underlying net assets
2. Portion of excess may be due to inventory
   Deduct from income in the first year (unless inventory not sold during year)
3. Portion of excess may be due to depreciable asset
   Divide by useful life and deduct from income each year
4. Portion of excess may be due to land
   No adjustment (unless land sold during year)
5. Remainder of excess attributed to goodwill
   Test each year for impairment and deduct from income if it has occurred

Application of Equity Method

Information given:

Investment	25%
Cost	$400,000
Book value of investee's underlying net assets	$900,000
Undervalued assets:	
Inventory	100,000
Building (20 years)	400,000
Land	200,000
Investee's unadjusted income	$225,000
Dividends	$40,000

Application of Equity Method (continued)

Information Applied

Value of investment—$ 400,000 ÷ 25%		$1,6000,000
Book value of underlying net assets		900,000
Difference (goodwill)		$ 700,000

Reconciliation of difference			*Earnings adjustment*
Inventory	$100,000		$100,000
Building	400,000	÷ 20	20,000
Land	200,000		
Total	$700,000		$120,000

Earnings			*Carrying value*	
Income reported by investee	$225,000		Cost	$400,000
Adjustments	(120,000)		+ Earnings	26,250
= Adjusted amount	105,000		− Dividends	
x % of ownership	25%		($40,000 × 25%)	10,000
= Investor's share	$26,250		= Carrying value	$416,250

Investments in Debt Securities

Valuation and Reporting of Debt Securities

	Trading	Available-for-sale (AFS)	Held-to-maturity (HTM)
Balance sheet classification	Current (typically) or noncurrent	Current or noncurrent	Noncurrent until maturity
Valuation	Fair value	Fair value	Amortized cost
Unrealized gains and losses	Income statement	Other comprehensive income	Not applicable

IFRS Investments

- Equity securities -FV through profit or loss or FV through OCI
- Debt securities only two classifications: Held-to-Maturity and FV through net income
- HTM valuationeffective interest rate based on estimated cash flow and estimated life (versus U.S. GAAP- contractual cash flows and contractual life)
- Available for sale (AFS)

An impairment loss on debt investment can be reversed if there is objective evidence

Transfers Between Classifications

Investments in Equity Securities

- Possible reason for changes from fair value to cost—Investment initially valued at FV may change because there is no longer a readily determinable FV
- Possible reason for changes from FV to equity method—Investor gains significant influence over the investee (or vice versa)
- Prospectively
- General rule—Transfers between classifications are accounted for at FV at the date of transfer

Investments in Debt Securities

- Possible reason for a change from held-to-maturity to fair value—Investor's ability to hold to maturity has changed
- Prospectively
- General rule—Transfers between classifications are accounted for at FV at the date of transfer

INTANGIBLE ASSETS

General Characteristics

Lack physical substance

Useful life extending more than one year from the balance sheet date

Associated with legal rights

Intangible Assets (continued)

Definite life intangibles

- Capitalize external costs
- Amortize; usually SL method

Indefinite life intangibles other than goodwill

- Capitalize external costs
- No amortization

Goodwill (also has indefinite life)

- Capitalize price of firm acquired less FV of net assets of firm acquired
- No amortization

Intangible Assets *(continued)*

Legal Costs of Defending an Intangible

- Successful—Capitalize legal costs as addition to carrying value of intangible
- Unsuccessful—Recognize legal costs as expense and write off intangible as a loss

Start-up Costs

Costs associated with start-up of organization should be immediately expensed.

Amortization

Straight-Line Amortization—Definite Life Intangibles (only)

Amortized over **shorter** of:

    Legal life

    Useful life

        DR: Amortization expense   xx

           CR: Intangible   xx

Impairment of Intangibles

Impairment—Definite Life Intangibles

- Tested for impairment when events suggest undiscounted future cash flow will be less than carrying value of intangible value
- Impairment if BV > Recoverable cost
- Impairment Loss = BV − FV

Impairment—Indefinite Life Intangibles Other than Goodwill

- Tested annually
- Impairment if BV > FV
- Impairment Loss = BV − FV

Goodwill

Acquisition

Must be part of (an acquisition) business combination

Measured as the excess of the FV of the acquired company as a whole over the FV of the identifiable net assets (Assets – Liabilities)

Internal Costs

May incur development or maintenance costs

All costs are expensed

Amortization

No amortization recorded

Private Company Standards

Allow goodwill to be amortized over a period not to exceed 10 years

Impairment of Goodwill

Must be tested for impairment at least annually or when certain circumstances indicate that its carrying value may be greater than its fair value. If so, perform the two-step impairment test:

1. Calculate and compare the fair value of the reporting unit to its carrying value

    a. If carrying value exceeds fair value, proceed to Step 2

2. Compare the implied fair value of the reporting unit goodwill to the carrying value

    a. Write down goodwill whenever implied fair value is less than carrying value

Subsequent reversal of a goodwill impairment loss is not permitted

Private Company Standards

A one-step approach used

Impairment occurs if the carrying amount of the entity/reporting unit (including goodwill) exceeds its fair value

Research and Development (R&D) Costs

Research—Aimed at discovery of new knowledge

New product or process

Improvement to existing product or process

Development—Converting new knowledge into plan or design

All R&D costs are expensed

If intangible assets purchased from others and tangible assets have alternative future uses, then asset is capitalized and amortized or depreciated as R&D expense

IFRS requires research costs to be expensed but allows capitalization of development costs if criteria are met

Research and Development (R&D) Costs (continued)

Items Included in R&D

1. Laboratory research
2. Conceptual formulation and design of possible products or process alternatives
3. Modification of the formulation or design of a product or process
4. Design, construction, and testing of preproduction prototypes and models
5. Design of tools, jigs, molds, and dies involving new technology
6. Design of a pilot plant

Research and Development (R&D) Costs (continued)

Items Excluded from R&D

1. Engineering follow-through
2. Quality control and routine testing
3. Troubleshooting
4. Adaptation of an existing capability to a particular customer's needs
5. Routine design of tools, jigs, molds, and dies
6. Legal work in connection with patent applications
7. Software development costs

Start-up Costs

Costs associated with start-up of organization should be immediately expensed

Franchises

Initial fee—Generally capitalized and amortized

Subsequent payments—Generally recognized as expense in period incurred

Internally Developed Software Costs

Expense—Costs incurred prior to the establishment of the technological feasibility

Capitalize and amortize—Costs incurred subsequent to the establishment of the technological feasibility

- Coding and testing
- Production of masters

Charge to inventory—Costs incurred during production

Internally Developed Software Costs (continued)

Timeline:

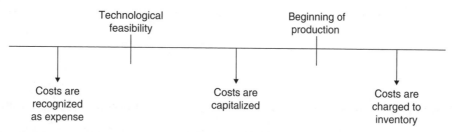

Internally Developed Software Costs (continued)

Amortization of capitalized software costs—Larger of:

Straight-line Method	or	**Revenue Method**

$$\frac{\text{Book value}}{\text{Remaining useful life}}$$
(Current period + Future periods)

$$\frac{\text{Current revenues} \times \text{Book value}}{\text{Total expected revenue}}$$
(Current revenues + Estimated future revenues)

Additional amortization:

Book value (after amortization) > Net realizable value (based on future revenues)

Book value is written down to net realizable value, with loss recognized

Under IFRS, software costs related to research are expensed, development costs are capitalized

Cloud Computing Software Costs

Criteria for Software License to Be Capitalized

1. Customer has contractual right to take possession of software at any time without significant penalty

2. Feasible for customer either to run software on its own or to contract with another unrelated party to the vendor to host software

Intangibles and IFRS

Under IFRS

- Intangibles can be revalued to fair value if there is an active market
- Reversal of impairment loss is permitted
- Estimated useful life and amortization method
- Goodwill is tested at the cash-generating-unit level; one-step test

Under U.S. GAAP

- Revaluation to fair value is not permitted
- Reversal of impairment loss is not allowed
- Estimated useful life and amortization method reviewed when events or circumstances change

Goodwill is tested at the reporting-unit level: a qualitative prestep and quantitative two-step test.

PAYABLES AND ACCRUED LIABILITIES

Current Liabilities

Liabilities due within one year of the balance sheet date or operating cycle, whichever is longer

- Valued at nominal amount (amount)
- Common examples include:
    - Accounts payable
    - Accrued liabilities
    - Deferred revenue
    - Income taxes payable
    - Dividends payable
    - Warranty obligations

Compensated Absences

Vacation pay, holiday pay, sick pay and other similar benefits must be accrued if all four criteria are met:

1. Past services of employees
2. Amounts vest or accumulate
3. Probable
4. Estimable

When all conditions met:

	Vest	**Accumulate**
Vacation pay	Must accrue	Must accrue
Sick pay	Must accrue	May accrue

Contingent Liabilities

Loss Contingencies

Probable—Accrue and disclose

- Not estimable—Disclose only
- Estimable within range—Accrue minimum of range (if no amount has a higher probability of occurring than any other amount)

Reasonably possible—Disclose only

Remote—Neither accrued nor disclosed

Gain Contingencies

- Never accrue (until realization occurs or is assured beyond reasonable doubt)
- May disclose

Warranty Liabilities

Warranty expense*

Sales
× % of warranty costs**
= Expense for period

Warranty liability

Estimated warranty liability

Payments	Beg. balance
	expense
	End balance

* When calculating warranty expense (for assurance-type warranties), the total estimated expense is recognized in the year of sale (e.g., Expected returns on year 1 sales = 2% in year of sale and 3% the year following the sale. Warranty expense would be calculated using 5%, matching all expenses to the period of the sale.)

** % of warranty costs = total expected percentage of defective units, for all years, multiplied by the total cost of repair/replacement.

Coupons

Discounts on Merchandise
Number of coupons not expired
× % expected to be redeemed

× Cost per coupon (face + service fee)
− Amount already paid
= Liability

Premiums (Prizes)
Number of units sold
× % expected to be redeemed
÷ Number required per prize
− Prizes already sent
× Cost per prize

= Liability

IFRS Contingencies

IFRS

Distinguishes between contingencies and provisions

Provisions are liabilities that are uncertain in timing or amount but is not of uncertain existence

- Probability threshold is more likely than not >50%—Accrue and disclose
- Estimable within a range—Accrue the midpoint of the range

Gain provisions recognized when virtually certain (in U.S. gain contingencies must be realized before recognition)

LONG-TERM DEBT (FINANCIAL LIABILITIES)

Notes Payable

Types of Notes Payable

1. Installment notes
2. Discounted notes
3. Notes—No stated interest rate

Current Notes Payable

- Reported at the amount due at maturity

Noncurrent Notes Payable

- Reported at PV of future payments, discounted at the prevailing interest rate at time of issuance

Notes Payable (continued)

Interest Recognition

- Effective method—Recognizes interest based on unpaid balance of debt
- Straight-line (SL) method—Recognizes same amount of interest and discount each period. Not appropriate for non-interest note when large difference between yield rate and stated rate

Bonds

Issuance—Interest Date

Cash (present value approach)*	xxx		
Discount or premium (plug)	xxx	or	xxx
Bonds payable (face amount)			xxx

*Cash amount = PV of principal + PV of interest payments (both use market rate)

Effective Interest Method—GAAP

Interest Payable
   Face amount
× Stated rate
× Portion of year since
   previous interest date
= Interest payable

Interest Expense
   Carrying value
× Yield rate
× Portion of year since
   previous interest date
= Interest expense

Difference
Amortization of discount or premium

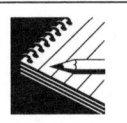

Straight-line Method—Not GAAP

Interest Payable
   Face amount
× Stated rate
× Portion of year since
   previous interest date
= Interest payable

Amortization
   Premium or discount
÷ Months in bond term
= Amortization per month
   interest date
× Months since last interest date
= Amortization

Interest expense = Interest payable ± Amortization

   + Amortization of discount
   − Amortization of premium

Recording Interest Expense

Interest expense	xxx		
Bond premium or discount (amortization)	xxx	or	xxx
Cash or interest payable			xxx

Issuance—Between Interest Dates

Cash proceeds*	xxx		
Discount or premium (plug)	xxx	or	xxx
Interest payable (interest amount)			xxx
Bonds payable (face)			xxx

*Proceeds = selling price of the bonds plus interest (at the stated rate) accrued since the last interest date

Issuance—Between Interest Dates (continued)

Interest

Calculated amount

Face amount of bonds
× Stated rate
× Portion of year since previous interest date
= Interest amount

Bond Issue Costs

Recorded as a reduction of the liability (shown as a contra account similar to a discount):

- Amortized over term of bond

Include legal fees, printing costs, and promotion costs related to the issuance

Refinancing Short-Term Obligations

To exclude from current liabilities—two requirements:

1. Company intends to refinance on a long-term basis
2. Company can demonstrate ability to refinance

The ability to refinance can be demonstrated in either of two ways:

1. Refinance on long-term basis after balance sheet date but before issuance
2. Enter into firm agreement with lender having ability to provide long-term financing
3. Issue equity securities replacing the debt

IFRS:

- Must have an agreement in place by the balance sheet date to exclude from current liabilities

Bond Retirement

Bond payable (face amount)	xxx		
Bond premium or discount (balance)	xxx	or	xxx
Gain or loss (plug)	xxx	or	xxx
Bond issue costs (balance)			xxx
Cash (amount paid)			xxx

Disclosures

A bond issuer should disclose:

- The face amount of bonds
- The nature and terms of the bonds including a discussion of credit and market risk, cash requirements, and related accounting policies
- The fair value of the bonds at the balance sheet date, indicated as a reasonable estimate of fair value

Troubled Debt

Troubled Debt Restructures (TDR) Overview

Type of TDR	Creditor	Debtor
TDR 1—Settlement	Accepts assets with market value < book value of debt, record a loss	Records a gain
TDR 2—Modification of terms: sum of new cash flows < book value of debt	Loan impairment	Gain; new debt book value = sum of new cash flows (no TVM)
TDR 2—Modification of terms: sum of new cash flows > book value of debt	Loan impairment	No gain; recognize interest at a lower rate

Distinguishing Liabilities from Equity

The FASB has adopted accounting standards that require certain items related to equity to be reported as liabilities. These items obligate the firm to deliver assets of a fixed monetary value, either cash or equity shares, in the future, and they include:

- Mandatorily redeemable shares
- Certain stock appreciation rights
- Financial instruments obligating the issuing firm to issue stock worth a fixed value. (By comparison, when the number of shares is fixed rather than the dollar amount, recorded as equity)
- Written put options and other financial instruments obligating the issuing firm to repurchase its own shares

Note that convertible shares whose conversion rate is not adjusted for changes in values do not fall into this category (e.g., preferred stock convertible at a fixed 10 for 1 ratio to the common stock would not be a liability).

Convertible Bonds

Recorded as bonds that are not convertible

Upon conversion:

Book Value Method				**Market Value Method**			
Bonds payable (face)	xx			Bonds payable (face)	xx		
Premium or discount (balance)	xx	or	xx	Premium or discount (balance)	xx	or	xx
Common stock (par)			xx	Common stock (par)			xx
Additional paid-in capital (APIC) (diff)			xx	APIC (computed)			xx
				Gain or loss (diff)	xx	or	xx

Convertible Bonds (continued)

Book Value Method

- Issuance price of stock = Carrying value of bonds
- No gain or loss

Market Value Method

- Issue price of stock = Fair value
- Gain or loss recognized

Detachable Warrants

Allocate proceeds using relative fair value method.

    Fair value of bonds (without warrants)

 +   Fair value of warrants (without bonds)

 =   Total fair value

Bonds = Proceeds × Value of bonds/Total value

Warrants = Proceeds × Value of warrants/Total value

Record issuance:

Cash (total proceeds)	xx		
Discount or premium (plug*)	xx	or	xx
APIC (amount allocated to warrants)			xx
Bonds payable (face amount)			xx

Bonds payable − Discount or plus premium = Amount allocated to bonds

---

IFRS

Under international standards, a financial instrument is classified as liability or equity, based on the substance of the transaction

1. If a financial instrument is an obligation to transfer cash or other financial assets, it is classified as a liability, regardless of form. It may be necessary to separate the liability and equity components as is the case with convertible bonds under international standards.

   - Financial instruments with characteristics of both debt and equity: *Compound instruments*
     - Convertible bonds and bonds with detachable warrants separated into components of debt and equity
     - Record liability component at fair value
     - Plug remaining value assigned to equity component

EQUITY

Issuance of Common Stock

Stock Issued for Cash, Property, or Services

Journal entry:

Cash, property, or expense (fair value)	xxx	
Common stock (par or stated value)		xxx
Additional paid-in capital (APIC) (difference)		xxx

Common Stock Subscribed

Subscription—Journal entry:

Cash (down payment)	xxx	
Subscriptions receivable (balance)	xxx	
Common stock subscribed (par or stated value)		xxx
APIC (difference)		xxx

Collection and issuance of shares—Journal entries:

Cash (balance)	xxx	
Subscriptions receivable		xxx
Common stock subscribed (par or stated value)	xxx	
Common stock (par or stated value)		xxx

Characteristics of Preferred Stock

Preference over common stock

- Receive dividends prior to common stockholders
- **Paid before common on liquidation**

Cumulative preferred stock

- Unpaid dividends accumulated as dividends in arrears
- Paid in subsequent periods prior to payment of current dividends to common or preferred
- Not considered liability until declared

Participating preferred stock

- Receive current dividends prior to common stockholders
- Receive additional dividends, in proportion to common stockholders, in periods of high dividends

Preferred Stock—Special Issuances

Preferred with Detachable Warrants

Cash (proceeds)	xxx	
APIC from warrants (amount allocated)		xxx
Preferred stock (par)		xxx
APIC from preferred stock (difference)		xxx

Amount allocated to warrants using relative fair value method:

    Fair value of warrants
+   Fair value of stock
=   Total fair value

Allocation:

- Fair value of warrants ÷ Total fair value × Proceeds = Amount allocated to warrants
- Fair value of stock ÷ Total fair value × Proceeds = Amount allocated to stock

Convertible Preferred Stock

Journal entry—Issuance

Cash (proceeds)	xxx	
Preferred stock (par)		xxx
APIC from preferred stock (difference)		xxx

Journal entry—Conversion

Preferred stock (par)	xxx	
APIC from preferred stock (original amount)	xxx	
Common stock (par or stated value)		xxx
APIC (difference)		xxx

Treasury Stock (TS)

Acquisition of Shares

Cost Method			Par Value Method		
TS (cost)	xx		TS (par value)	xx	
Cash		xx	APIC-common stock	xx	
			RE (difference)	xx	
			or		
			APIC from TS (difference)		xx
			Cash (cost)		xx

Treasury Stock (TS) (continued)

Reissuance of Shares

Sale—more than cost:

Cost Method			Par Value Method		
Cash (proceeds)	xx		Cash (proceeds)	xx	
TS (cost)		xx	TS (par)		xx
APIC from TS		xx	APIC-common		xx
			(difference)		

Sale—less than cost:

Cost Method			Par Value Method
Cash (proceeds)	xx		Same entry as above
APIC from TS (difference up to balance)	xx		
RE (remainder of difference)	xx		
TS (cost)		xx	

Focus on
Equity

Dividends

Cash Dividends

Recorded when declared

1. Dividends in arrears to preferred stockholders if cumulative
2. Normal current dividend to preferred stockholders
3. Comparable current dividend to common stockholders
4. Remainder
   - Allocated between common and preferred shares if preferred stock is participating
   - Paid to common stockholders if preferred stock is nonparticipating

Property Dividends

Journal entry

Retained earnings (fair value of property)	xxx	
Gain (or loss)	xxx or	xxx
Asset (carrying value of property)		xxx

Liquidating Dividends

Journal entry

Retained earnings (balance)	xxx	
APIC (plug)	xxx	
Cash or dividends payable		xxx

Stock Dividends

Journal entry—Normal stock dividend, usually 20% or less

Retained earnings (fair value of stock issued)	xxx	
Common stock (par or stated value)		xxx
APIC (difference)		xxx

Journal entry—Large stock dividend, usually more than 25%

Retained earnings (par or stated value)	xxx	
Common stock (par or stated value)		xxx

Stock Splits

- A stock spit is not a dividend
- No journal entry required
- Increases number of shares outstanding and decreases the par or stated value
- Equity accounts not affected
- Reduces market price

Stock Splits Effected in Form of Dividend

- If treated as a stock split effected in the form of a stock dividend, APIC-common is debited rather than retained earnings

Retained Earnings

Appropriations

Set up to disclose to financial statement users future commitments that are not subject to accrual.

Journal entry:

Retained earnings	xxx	
Retained earnings appropriated for…		xxx

When the commitment is met, accrued, or avoided, the appropriation is reversed.

Journal entry:

Retained earnings appropriated for…	xxx	
Retained earnings		xxx

Prior-Period Adjustments

Made to correct errors in financial statements of prior periods

Adjustment to beginning retained earnings

- Equal to net amount of errors from periods prior to earliest period presented
- Reduced by tax effect

Presented on statement of retained earnings

- Unadjusted beginning balance reported
- Increased or decreased for prior-period adjustment
- Result is adjusted beginning balance

Statement of Retained Earnings

Beginning retained earnings, as previously reported	xxx	
±	Prior period adjustments	<u>xxx</u>
=	Beginning retained earnings, as adjusted	xxx
+	Net income for period	xxx
−	Dividends	xxx
−	Appropriations	xxx
+	Appropriations eliminated	<u>xxx</u>
=	Ending retained earnings	<u><u>xxx</u></u>

IFRS and Owner's Equity

- Unlike U.S. GAAP, statement of changes in owners' equity required

Book Value per Share

Calculation:

Total stockholders' equity
- − Preferred stock (par value or liquidation preference)
- − Dividends in arrears on cumulative preferred stock
- = Stockholders' equity attributable to common stockholders
- ÷ Common shares outstanding at balance sheet date
- = Book value per common share

Quasi Reorganizations

Allows a firm with negative retained earnings to "start fresh" and begin paying dividends

Three Steps:

1. Write assets down to market value, further reducing retained earnings (increasing the deficit)
2. Reduce contributed capital to absorb the retained earnings deficit
3. Change value/number of shares—If needed, change par value or the number of shares of common stock to absorb the remaining deficit

Journal entry:

Common stock (reduction in par value)	xxx	
APIC (plug)	xxx or xxx	
Retained earnings (eliminate deficit)		xxx
Assets (eliminate overstatements)		xxx

Disclosure of Information about Capital Structure

Rights and privileges of various debt and equity securities outstanding:

- Number of shares of common and preferred stock authorized, issued, and outstanding
- Dividend and liquidation preferences
- Participation rights
- Call prices and dates
- Conversion or exercise prices or rates and pertinent dates
- Sinking fund requirements
- Unusual voting rights
- Significant terms of contracts to issue additional shares

Reporting Stockholders' Equity

6% cumulative preferred stock, $100 par value, 200,000 shares authorized, 120,000 shares issued and outstanding		$12,000,000
Common stock, $10 par value, 1,500,000 shares authorized, 1,150,000 shares issued and 1,090,000 shares outstanding		11,500,000
Additional paid-in capital		3,650,000
		27,150,000
Retained Earnings:		
Unappropriated	$6,925,000	
Retained earnings appropriated for plant expansion	1,400,000	8,325,000
Accumulated other comprehensive income:		
Accumulated unrealized gain due to increase value of marketable securities available for sale		
Accumulated translation adjustment	(515,000)	235,000
Less: Treasury stock, 60,000 shares at cost		780,000
Total Stockholders' Equity		$34,930,000

Focus on
Equity

205

REVENUE RECOGNITION

Revenues

Inflows or other enhancements of assets of an entity or settlements of its liabilities (or a combination of the two) from delivering or producing goods, rendering services, or other activities that constitute the entity's ongoing major or central operations

Five Steps of Revenue Recognition

Step 1. Identify the contract with a customer.

Step 2. Identify the performance obligation(s) in the contract.

Step 3. Determine the transaction price.

Step 4. Allocate the transaction price to the performance obligation(s) in the contract.

Step 5. Recognize revenue when the entity satisfies the performance obligation(s).

Determining Transaction Price

Transaction price in a contract may be impacted by the following:

- **Variable consideration**—A contract includes pricing terms that will be impacted or determined by a future event
  - **Expected value method**—Uses sum of probability-weighted outcomes to determine the transaction price (use when an entity has many contracts with similar characteristics)
  - **Most likely amount method**—Uses the most likely outcome to determine the amount of revenue to recognize (use when an entity has two possible outcomes)
- **Significant financing component**—Contracts that allow the buyer to pay at a much later date (more than one year) and include both sales revenue and interest revenue
- **Noncash consideration**—When consideration received is in a form other than cash; seller recognizes revenue at an amount that reflects fair value of the noncash consideration received
- **Consideration payable to customer**—Contract terms may include discounts or rebates

Allocating Transaction Price

Single Performance Obligation—Contracts cover a single performance obligation to which the entire transaction price is assigned.

Dr. Cash or Accounts Receivable	xxx	
Cr. Sales Revenue		xxx
Dr. Cost of Goods Sold	xxx	
Cr. Inventory		xxx

Multiple Performance Obligations—Contracts include more than one performance obligation but list only one transaction price.

Step 1—**Identify the separate performance obligations**

Step 2—**Allocate the transaction price to each performance obligation.**

If the stand-alone selling price is not directly observable, then estimate the stand-alone selling price.

Special Issues in Revenue Recognition

Warranties

Assurance-type warranties—Warranties that offer the customer assurance that the product will function to agreed-upon specifications

- Not considered a separate performance obligation

Service-type warranties—Warranties that provide service in addition to assurance

- Considered separate performance obligations
- Portion of transaction price is allocated to warranty
- For extended (service-type) warranty, unearned revenue is recognized as revenue over the life of contract; warranty expense recognized as incurred

Warranties are accounted for as separate performance obligations when the customer has the option to purchase as a distinct service separate from the product and the warranty provides a service in addition to promises under assurance-type warranties.

Sales with a Right of Return

- Not accounted for as a performance obligation
- Recognize revenue for the amount expected

Nonrefundable Up-Front Fees

- Most represent an advance payment for goods or services that will be provided in the future
- Revenue recognized as goods or services are provided

Bill-and-Hold Arrangements

- Seller may recognize revenue before transferring goods to the buyer if buyer has control of goods and certain criteria are met

Contract Modifications

A new separate contract results if modification is for new or additional promised goods or services that are distinct; and consideration for the new or additional goods or services reflects stand-alone prices.

- Accounted for separate from existing contract

An existing contract is modified if products or services covered by the modification are not distinct from the existing contract's products or services or if products or services are not priced at a stand-alone selling price.

- Accounted for using a prospective approach

DEFERRED COMPENSATION

Pensions

Defined Contribution Plans

The amount of the employer contribution is defined by contract.

Defined Benefit Pension Plan

The benefits paid during retirement are based on a formula and therefore are defined.

Projected Benefit Obligation (PBO)

PV of unpaid pension benefits promised for work done through the balance sheet date, as measured by the benefit formula

Pension Expense

Service cost (debit)

\+ Interest cost (debit)

\- Expected returns on plan assets (typically, CPA exam assumes positive returns, so credit)

± Amortization of prior service cost (debit)

± Amortization of net gain or loss

\= Pension expense reported in operating income

Pension Expense (continued)

Service cost—Increase in pension expense resulting from services performed by employees

Interest—Beginning PBO × Discount (interest) rate

Expected return on plan assets—(Expected rate of return) × (Plan assets at Jan. 1 at market value)

Amortization of net gain or loss—Two components:

1. Difference between actual and expected returns on plan assets
2. Changes in PBO caused by estimate changes or experience changes

Report on balance sheet difference between fair value of plan assets and the PBO as a noncurrent asset if overfunded and a noncurrent liability if underfunded in a pension asset/liability account

Pension Expense Entries

If expense equals cash payment:

Pension expense	xxx	
Cash		xxx

If pension expense is greater than cash payment:

Pension expense	xxx	
Pension asset/liability		xxx
Cash		xxx

If pension expense is less than cash payment:

Pension expense	xxx	
Pension asset/liability		xxx
Cash		xxx

U.S. GAAP—IFRS Differences

- PBO for U.S. standards is called defined benefit obligation (DBO) for international standards
- Pension liability or asset reported on balance sheet (for U.S.) is called defined benefit liability or asset (for IFRS).
- PSC is prior service cost for U.S., but is called past-service cost for IFRS
- For IFRS, pension expense reported in separate components rather than a single amount on the income statement. Components are: service cost (including past service cost), and net interest cost (interest cost netted against expected return).
- Pension gains/losses for U.S. are called "remeasurement gains/losses" for IFRS

Disclosures for Defined Contribution Plans

- Pension expense presented separately from defined benefit plan pension expense
- Description of the plan
- Description of significant changes during period affecting comparability
- Reconciliation of beginning and ending pension liability balance

Disclosures for Defined Benefit Plans

- Pension expense and components
- Funded status (pension liability)
- Reconciliation of beginning and ending balances for projected benefit obligation (PBO) including service cost, interest cost, gains and losses, amendments and other changes; and for plan assets including contributions, benefits, and other changes
- Accumulated benefit obligation (ABO) and vested benefit obligation (VBO)
- Any settlements or curtailments
- Estimates and assumptions including benefits expected to be paid in each of the next five years, employer contributions expected to be paid in the next 12 months, discount rates, rate of compensation increase, and expected long-term rate of return on plan assets
- Amounts recognized in other comprehensive income (OCI) and reclassification adjustments, and OCI amounts not yet recognized in pension expense

Postretirement Benefits

Types of Benefits

Company pays for:

- Health care
- Tuition assistance
- Legal services
- Life insurance
- Day care
- Housing subsidies

Individuals covered:

- Retired employees
- Beneficiaries
- Covered dependents

Postretirement Benefit Expense

Service cost (debit)

+ Interest (debit)

− Expected return on assets (CPA exam assumes positive returns, so credit)

± Amortization of prior service cost (debit)

± Amortization of net gain or loss at January 1

± Amortization of transition obligation

= Postretirement benefit expense

SHARE-BASED PAYMENTS

Stock Purchase Plan

Noncompensatory when:

- Essentially all employees can participate
- Employee must decide within one month of firm setting price of stock whether to enroll
- Discount does not exceed employer cost savings inherent in issuing directly to employees ($\leq$5% market price meets this criterion)
- Purchase price must be based solely on the market price of the stock
- Employees can cancel enrollment before purchase date and obtain full refund

If noncompensatory; Compensation expense = Amount paid by employer

Compensatory when:

- All criteria are not met

If compensatory; Compensation expense = Amount paid by employer plus discount

Stock Option Plans

- Compensatory
- Options must be accounted for using FV at date of grant based on option pricing model (including Black-Scholes, lattice, and others)
- Compensation expense = FV of options expected to be exercised
- Total compensation expense amortized SL over service period
- Adjusted for forfeitures (either as occur or estimated) in current period and prospectively

IFRS and Stock Options

- In U.S. GAAP, increase in deferred tax assets for a stock award or stock option plan based on cumulative compensation expense to date. That amount is used as the estimate of the future tax deduction and is the basis for increasing the deferred tax asset.
- Under IFRS deferred tax assets increase only when option has intrinsic value (market price > option price) during the service period
- Graded vesting—under U.S. GAAP, a simplified straight-line method can be chosen. For IFRS the straight-line method is not allowed.

Stock Awards

- Stock is restricted until award vests.
- Vesting or service period can be one or more years.
- Manager pays nothing for award.
- Total compensation expense = FV of stock at grant date
- Compensation expense (and APIC) recognized over service period.
- If award does not vest, expense is reversed.
- Adjustments to compensation expense occur in current period and prospectively.

Stock Appreciation Rights

Calculating liability if cash is to be paid

    Stock price
    −   Amount specified in stock appreciation rights
    =   Amount per share
    ×   # of stock appreciation rights
    =   Total liability
    ×   Portion of service period elapsed
    =   Liability on balance sheet date

Amount needed to increase or decrease liability is recognized as compensation expense

INCOME TAXES

Income Tax Basics
(*Accounting for Income Taxes*—ASC 740)

Income Tax Expense—income tax liability plus or minus the net change in the deferred tax accounts for the period (for the year's transactions)

Taxable income = Pretax accounting income

No temporary or permanent differences

- Income tax expense = Current income tax expense
- No deferred tax effect

Taxable income ≠ Pretax accounting income

- Temporary and/or permanent differences
- Income tax expense = Current income tax expense ± Deferred income tax expense

---

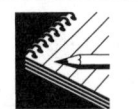

Current Income Tax

Current income tax expense = Taxable income × Current tax rate

Current tax liability = Current income tax expense − Estimated payments

Taxable income:

> Pretax accounting income (financial statement income)
> ±   Permanent differences
> ±   Changes in cumulative amounts of temporary differences
> =   Taxable income

Permanent and Temporary Differences

Permanent differences

- Nontaxable income (interest income on municipal bonds) and nondeductible expenses (premiums on officers' life insurance)
- No income tax effect

Temporary differences

- Timing difference—only difference between GAAP and tax is timing recognition
- Carrying values of assets or liabilities $\neq$ Tax bases
- May be taxable temporary differences (TTD) or deductible temporary differences (DTD)
- TTD result in deferred tax liabilities, and DTD result in deferred tax assets

Assets

- Financial statement basis > Tax basis = TTD
- Financial statement basis < Tax basis = DTD

Permanent and Temporary Differences (continued)

Liabilities

- Financial statement basis > Tax basis = DTD
- Financial statement basis < Tax basis = TTD

Often it is easier to examine the net effect on income. For example, if straight-line depreciation is used for financial statement purposes and the modified accelerated cost recovery system (MACRS) is used for tax purposes, depreciation expense for book purposes < that for tax purposes leading to net financial income > net taxable income, resulting in a deferred tax liability.

- Net financial income > Net taxable income = Deferred tax liability
- Net financial income < Net taxable income = Deferred tax asset

Deferred Tax Assets and Liabilities

TTD × Enacted future tax rate = Deferred tax liability

DTD × Enacted future tax rate = Deferred tax asset

Selecting appropriate rate:

1. Determine future period when temporary difference will have tax effect (period of reversal)
2. Determine enacted tax rate for that period

Balance Sheet Presentation

Deferred tax assets (and associated valuation allowances) and deferred tax liabilities are all classified as noncurrent

For balance sheet reporting, the net of the noncurrent DTA and DTL, as well as any related valuation allowance, is reported as one net noncurrent asset or liability

Deferred Income Tax Expense or Benefit

1. Calculate balances of deferred tax liabilities and assets and valuation allowances
2. Combine into single net amount
3. Compare to combined amount at beginning of period

   - Increase in net liability amount = Deferred income tax expense
   - Decrease in net asset amount = Deferred income tax expense
   - Increase in net asset amount = Deferred income tax benefit
   - Decrease in net liability amount = Deferred income tax benefit

Valuation Allowance for Deferred Tax Assets

May apply to any deferred tax asset

- If it is more likely than not that some or all of deferred tax asset will not be realized
- Treated as a negative deferred tax asset account

Valuation allowance = Portion of deferred tax asset that will not be realized

IFRS for Deferred Income Taxes

- Use enacted rate or substantially enacted rate
- No valuation allowance (reported net)

Uncertain Tax Positions

- Applies to all tax positions related to income taxes subject to ASC 740
- Utilizes a two-step approach for evaluating tax positions
  - Recognition (Step 1) occurs when an enterprise concludes that the uncertain tax position, based solely on its technical merits, is more likely than not to be sustained upon examination.
  - Measurement (Step 2) is only addressed if Step 1 has been maintained. Under Step 2, the tax benefit is measured as the largest amount of benefit, determined on a cumulative probability basis, that is more likely than not to be realized (i.e., a likelihood of occurrence greater than 50%).

Uncertain Tax Positions (continued)

- If tax positions fail to qualify for initial recognition under Step 1, then income tax expense is not reduced and an additional tax liability is recognized
- ASC 740/FIN 48 specifically prohibits the use of a deferred tax valuation allowance as a substitute for derecognition of tax positions.

Net Operating Losses (NOL)

- Carryback (CB) election—2 years
- Carryforward (CF) election—20 years
- Income tax benefit in year of NOL
- Value of CB or CF—the tax saved, not the actual loss

ACCOUNTING CHANGES AND ERROR CORRECTIONS

Change in Accounting Principle: Allowed Only if Required by New Accounting Principles or Change to Preferable Method

Use retrospective application of new principle:

1. Calculate revised balance of asset or liability as of beginning of period as if new principle had always been in use.
2. Compare balance to amount reported under old method.
3. Multiply difference by 100% minus tax rate.
4. Result is treated on books as prior-period adjustment to beginning retained earnings.
5. All previous periods being presented in comparative statements restated to new principle.

Change in Accounting Principle (continued)

6. Beginning balance of retained earnings in the year of the change is adjusted to reflect the use of the new principle through that date.

7. IFRS: Similar rules—Voluntary change must provide more reliable and relevant information. Terminology differences are present between IFRS and U.S. GAAP

Journal entry:

Asset or liability	xxx	
Retained earnings*		xxx
Current or deferred tax liability (asset)		xxx

or

Retained earnings*	xxx	
Current or deferred tax liability (asset)	xxx	
Asset or liability		xxx

*Cumulative effect of accounting change (closed to retained earnings)

Prospective Application

- No retrospective application
- Change applied as of beginning of current period
- Applied in current and future periods

Change in Estimate

- Derived from new information and is a change that causes the carrying amount of an asset or liability to change, or that changes the subsequent accounting for an asset or liability
- Now also includes changing method of depreciation, amortization, or depletion
- In general, when a change in principle cannot be distinguished from a change in estimate, the change is treated as a change in estimate (prospectively)

Accounting Errors—Restatement

Applies to:

- Change from unacceptable principle to acceptable principle
- Errors in prior period financial statements
- Change in estimate based on negligence or in bad faith are also error corrections

Reporting of a prior period adjustment (PPA):

1. If beginning RE is incorrect, then record a PPA in a journal entry
2. If the earliest RE balance is incorrect, then PPA must be reported in the retained earnings statement

Errors Affecting Income

Error (Ending balance)

	Current Statement	Prior Statement
Asset overstated	Overstated	No effect
Asset understated	Understated	No effect
Liability overstated	Understated	No effect
Liability understated	Overstated	No effect

Error (Beginning balance — Ending balance is correct)

Asset overstated	Understated	Overstated
Asset understated	Overstated	Understated
Liability overstated	Overstated	Understated
Liability understated	Understated	Overstated

Errors Affecting Income (continued)

Error (Beginning balance—Ending balance is not correct)

	Current Statement	**Prior Statement**
Asset overstated	No effect	Overstated
Asset understated	No effect	Understated
Liability overstated	No effect	Understated
Liability understated	No effect	Overstated

BUSINESS COMBINATIONS

Business Combination Overview

Business combination—Transaction or event where an entity obtains control of a business

Legal Forms of Business Combinations

1. Merger—One preexisting entity acquires either a group of assets that constitute a business or a controlling equity interest of another preexisting entity and "collapses" the acquired assets or entity into the acquiring entity.
   - Acquisition method; reported as a single entity
2. Consolidation—A new entity consolidates the net assets or the equity interests of two (or more) preexisting entities
   - Acquisition method; carried at cost or equity; reported as consolidated statements
3. Acquisition—One preexisting entity acquires controlling equity interest of another preexisting entity, but both continue to exist and operate as separate legal entities.
   - Acquisition method; carried at cost or equity; reported as consolidated statements

Push-Down Accounting

The acquiree has the option to apply pushdown accounting anytime there is a change in control as defined in ASC 805 and 810

If the acquiree elects to apply pushdown accounting, it would revalue all of the assets and liabilities to acquisition date fair value as determined by the acquirer in its application of ASC 805

The entry is made directly on the books to the subsidiary

Has no effect on the presentation of the consolidated financial statements or separate parent financial statements

The subsidiary's financial statements would be recorded at fair value rather than historical cost

IFRS Business Combinations

- Focus is on the concept of the power to control, with control being the parent's ability to govern the financial and operating policies of an entity to obtain benefits. Control is presumed to exist if parent owns more than 50% of the votes, and potential voting rights must be considered.
- Special-purpose entities
    - IFRS: Consolidated when the substance of the relationship indicates that an entity controls the SPE
- Consolidated financial statements required except when parent is a wholly owned subsidiary
- Equity method Investments must use equity method (i.e., no fair value option)
- Joint ventures can use either equity method or proportionate consolidation method
- Push-down accounting not allowed

FINANCIAL INSTRUMENTS

Risk of Loss

Market risk—Losses due to fluctuations in marketplace

Credit risk—Losses due to nonperformance of other party

Concentration of credit risk—Several instruments have common characteristics, resulting in similar risks

Investments in Derivative Securities

Derivatives—Derive their value from other assets. Examples:

- Stock option—Value based on underlying stock price
- Commodity futures contract—Value based on underlying commodity price

Initially recorded at cost (or allocated amount)—Reported on balance sheet at fair value

Characteristics of Derivatives

Settlement in cash or assets easily convertible to cash (such as marketable securities)

Underlying index on which value of derivative is based (usually the price of some asset)

No or little net investment at time of creation:

- Futures-based derivative involves no payments at all when derivative created

  - Such a derivative must be settled on settlement date in all cases

- Options-based derivative involves small premium payment when derivative created

  - Option holder has right not to settle derivative if results would be unfavorable
  - Payment of premium when derivative created is price of this option

Hedging

Speculative—Attempt to profit from favorable change in underlying index

- Gain or loss on change in fair value reported in ordinary income

Hedge accounting—Certain derivatives qualify as hedge instruments and must meet the following criteria:

- Sufficient documentation must be provided at designation
- The hedge must be highly effective throughout its life
    - It must have the ability to generate changes measured quarterly and whenever earnings or financial statements are reported (minimum)
    - It must move in the opposite direction to the offsetting item
    - The cumulative change in value of the hedging instrument should be between 80% and 125% of offsetting item
    - The method assessing effectiveness must be consistent with risk management approach
    - Similar hedges should be assessed similarly
- If a hedge is not 100% effective, the ineffective portion must be reported in current earnings

Hedging (continued)

Fair value hedge—Attempt to offset risk of existing asset, liability, or commitment

- Gain or loss on change in derivative reported in ordinary income

  - Should approximately offset loss or gain on item being hedged

Cash flow hedge—Attempt to offset risk associated with future expected transactions

- Gain or loss from effective portion excluded from ordinary income until offsetting future event affects income

  - Reported as part of other comprehensive income until that time

Foreign currency hedge—Attempt to offset exposure to foreign currencies

- Gain or loss reported in current earnings or other comprehensive income depending on type of foreign currency hedge (As fair value hedge—gains and losses to net income; As cash flow hedge—gains and losses for effective portion to OCI and for ineffective portion to net income)

Required Disclosures

- Fair value
- Off-balance-sheet credit risk—Credit risk that is not already reflected as an accrued contingency
- Concentration of credit risk
- Hedging disclosures

  - Objective and strategies
  - Context to understand instrument
  - Risk management policies
  - A list of hedged instruments
  - Instruments designated as fair value hedges, cash flow hedges, hedges of foreign currency exposure of net investments in foreign operations, and any other derivatives

IFRS Derivatives

- Definition of a derivative does not include a notional amount
- Embedded derivatives—assessed only at initiation of contract
- Embedded derivatives within a single host separated as multiple derivatives
- Foreign exchange risk associated with business combination can be hedged
- Part-term hedges are permitted

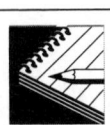

Private Company Standards

May use simplified hedge accounting for swaps that convert a variable-rate borrowing to a fixed rate borrowing

Qualifying swaps may be measured at settlement value

May choose to use the annual report available to be issued date to designate a hedge versus the hedge inception date

FOREIGN CURRENCY DENOMINATED TRANSACTIONS

Foreign Currency

Foreign Currency Import and Export Transactions

Receivable (export) or payable (import)

- Record at **spot rate** (exchange rate at the current date)
- Adjust to new spot rate on each financial statement date

Journal entry:

Receivable or payable	xxx	
Foreign currency transaction gain		xxx
OR		
Foreign currency transaction loss	xxx	
Receivable or payable		xxx

Gain or loss = Change in spot rate × Receivable or payable (in foreign currency)

Introduction to Forward and Option Contracts

FX forward (futures) contracts—establish an obligation to buy or sell a foreign currency

FX options contracts—establish a right to buy or sell a foreign currency, but not the obligation to do so

General Accounting Requirements

- Measure at fair value
- Changes in fair value result in gains and losses
- Treatment of gains and losses depends on the purpose of forward contract
    1. Economic (natural) hedge or speculation—gains/losses recognized in net income.
    2. Qualified hedge—depends on nature of hedge:
        - Cash flow hedge—effective portion other comprehensive income
        - Fair value hedge—net income

Conversion of Financial Statements

Conversion to U.S. $:

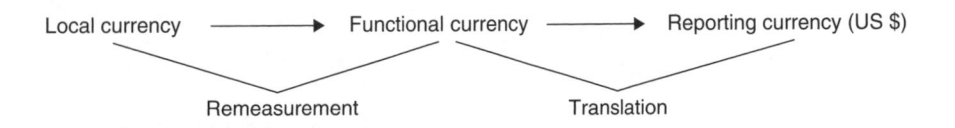

CONVERSION TO U.S. $:

Local currency   ⟶   Functional currency   ⟶   Reporting currency (US $)

Remeasurement   Translation

Functional currency—Currency of primary economic environment in which entity operates.

1. Functional currency = Local currency
   - Translate from local currency to U.S. $
2. Functional currency = U.S. $
   - Remeasure from local currency to U.S. $
3. Functional currency neither local currency nor U.S. $
   - Remeasure from local currency to functional currency
   - Translate from functional currency to U.S. $

Conversion Using Remeasurement and Translation

Remeasurement (Temporal Method)

Historical rate:

Nonmonetary assets and liabilities

Contributed capital accounts

Revenue and expense accounts related to nonmonetary items/significant transactions that occur on one date

Current rate:

Monetary assets and liabilities

All other revenue, expense, gain, and loss items (weighted)

Weighted average:

Revenues and expenses occurring evenly throughout the year

Retained earnings is computed

Difference:

Remeasurement gain or loss

Reported on income statement

Translation (Current Rate Method)

Convert most BS accounts using current exchange rate

Retained earnings is computed

Items occurring on one date and paid-in-capital use historic rate

Convert IS accounts (revenues, expenses, gains, and losses) using:

Weighted-average rate for period, or

Exchange rate at date item earned or incurred

Difference:

Translation gain or loss

Component of stockholders' equity

Excluded from net income
Included in comprehensive income

Focus on

Foreign Currency Denominated Transactions

LEASES

Accounting for Leases

Determining Type of Lease

Do rights and risks of ownership transfer from lessor to lessee?

Yes

Capital lease

No

Operating lease

Operating Leases

Lessor Accounting

Rent revenue

Various expenses (depreciation on asset, taxes, insurance, and maintenance)

Lessee Accounting

Rent expense

Miscellaneous expenses (taxes, insurance, and maintenance)

Rent Revenue or Expense

- Recognized uniformly over lease (straight-line basis)
- Total of rents over term of lease ÷ Number of periods (lease term) = Rent per period

Leasehold Improvements

Intangible asset for lessee

Amortize over shorter of:

- Useful life
- Remaining term of lease

Improvements made in place of rent are expensed in period incurred

Capital Leases—Lessee

Transfer of Rights and Risks of Ownership—At Least One of Four Criteria

Actual transfer

    Criterion 1—Title transfers to lessee by end of term

    Criterion 2—Lease contains bargain purchase option

Transfer in substance

    Criterion 3—Lease term $\geq$ 75% of useful life

    Criterion 4—Present value of minimum lease payments $\geq$ 90% of fair value of leased asset at inception

To calculate present value, lessee uses lower of:

- Incremental borrowing rate
- Rate implicit in lease (if known)

Inception of Lease

Journal entry of lessee to record lease:

Leased asset	xxx	
Lease obligation		xxx

Amount of asset and liability = Present value (PV) of minimum lease payments:

- Payments beginning at inception result in annuity due
- Payments beginning at end of first year result in ordinary annuity
- Payments include bargain purchase option or guaranteed residual value (lump sum at end of lease)
- Lessee uses lower of implicit interest rate or lessee's borrowing rate.

Lease payments

Payment at inception:

Lease obligation	xxx	
Cash		xxx

Subsequent payments:

Interest expense	xxx	
Lease obligation	xxx	
Cash		xxx

Interest amount:

Balance in lease obligation
$\times$ Interest rate (used to calculate PV)
$\times$ Time since last payment (usually one year)
$=$ Interest amount

Periodic Expenses—Depreciation

Actual transfer

- Life = Useful life of property
- Salvage value taken into consideration

Transfer in substance

- Life = Shorter of useful life or lease term
- No salvage value

Periodic Expenses—Executory Costs

Consist of insurance, maintenance, and taxes

Recognized as expense when incurred

Capital Leases—Lessor

Rights and risks of ownership transfer from lessor to lessee?

Yes

No

Additional criteria

Operating lease

Transfer of Rights and Risks of Ownership—At Least One of Four Criteria

- Same criteria as lessee
- To calculate PV, lessor uses rate implicit in lease

Additional Criteria

- Collectibility of lease payments reasonably predictable
- No significant uncertainties as to costs to be incurred in connection with lease

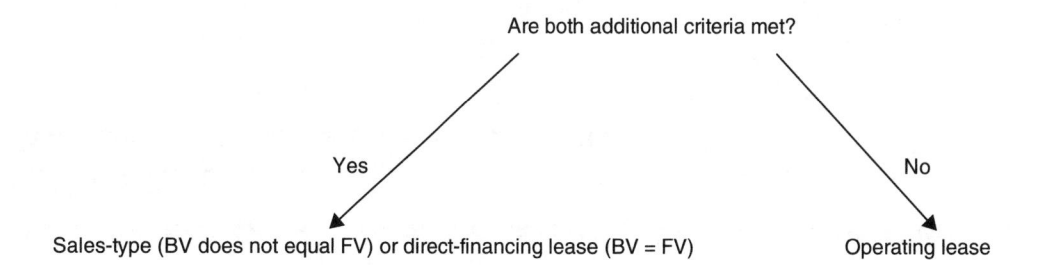

Are both additional criteria met?

Yes

No

Sales-type (BV does not equal FV) or direct-financing lease (BV = FV)

Operating lease

Direct-Financing Leases

Inception of Lease

Journal entry to record lease:

Receivable	xxx	
Accumulated depreciation (if any)	xxx	
Asset		xxx
Unearned interest revenue		xxx

Receivable = Sum of minimum lease payments + Any unguaranteed residual (gross method)

Asset and accumulated depreciation—To remove carrying value of asset from lessor's books (FV = Cost value)

Unearned interest = Total interest over term

Collections—Direct-Financing Leases

Recognition of periodic interest revenue:

Cash	xxx	
Unearned interest	xxx	
Interest revenue (formula)		xxx
Receivable		xxx

Interest amount:

Beginning net lease receivable
$\times$ Interest rate (implicit in lease)
$\times$ Time since last payment (usually 1 year)
$=$ Interest amount

Sales-Type Leases (STL)

In an STL, the book value of the lessor's asset is not equal to (usually less than) its fair value.

Inception of Lease

Lessor journal entry to record lease:

Lease receivable	xxx	
Cost of goods sold	xxx	
Unearned interest		xxx
Sales		xxx
Asset		xxx

Receivable = Sum of minimum lease payments + Any unguaranteed residual

Cost of goods sold = Cost of asset

Unearned interest revenue = Total interest over term books

Sales = Fair value/Selling price

Asset = Cost of asset

Collections

Journal entry to record accrued interest:

Unearned interest	xxx	
Interest revenue (formula)		xxx

Journal entry at payment date:

Cash	xxx	
Receivable		xxx

IFRS Lease Rules

- IFRS—Key issue: Look at economic substance to determine if substantially all benefits/risks of ownership are transferred.
- Two types of leases: Finance or operating

  - If any of the following is met, then it is a finance lease. Note: No 75% or 90% test.

    1. Title transfer (same as U.S.)
    2. Bargain purchase option (same as U.S.)
    3. The lease term is for the major part of the remaining economic life of the asset (U.S. uses 75%).
    4. The present value of the minimum lease payments at the inception of the lease is at least equal to substantially all of the fair value of the leased asset (U.S. uses 90% or more).
    5. The leased assets are of a specialized nature such that only the lessee can use them without modifications.

Sale-Leasebacks

Major Leaseback

PV of minimum lease payments is $\geq$ 90% of the asset's fair value

- Capital lease—record gain in contra-leased asset account and amortize as reduction in depreciation expense in same proportion as depreciation expense recognized
- Operating lease—record gain in liability account and amortize as reduction in rent expense

Minor Leaseback

PV of minimum lease payments $\leq$ 10% of fair value of property sold

- Sale and leaseback recognized as separate transactions
- Gain or loss on sale recognized immediately

Less than Major but More than Minor Leaseback

(90% of fair value) > (present value of minimum lease payments) > (10% of fair value)

- The lessee defers and amortizes gain to the extent that it exceeds the present value of the minimum lease payments
- Gain up to PV of minimum lease payments recognized in period of sale

Balance Sheet Presentation

Leased asset

- Reported as property, plant, and equipment (PP&E)
- Reported net of accumulated depreciation

Lease obligation

- Current liability = Principal payments due in subsequent period
- Noncurrent liability = Remainder

Disclosures—Lessee

- Gross amount of assets recorded under capital leases
- Minimum lease payments for each of next five years and in aggregate
- Description of leasing activities

NOT-FOR-PROFIT ORGANIZATIONS

Not-for-profit organizations include:

- Hospitals
- Colleges and universities
- Voluntary health and welfare organizations (VHWO)

Required financial statements for all types include:

1. Statement of Financial Position
2. Statement of Activities
3. Statement of Cash Flows

Statement of Financial Position

Includes assets, liabilities, and net assets

- Net assets with donor restrictions—The part of net assets of a not-for-profit entity that is subject to donor-imposed restrictions (donors include other types of contributors, including makers of certain grants)
- Net assets without donor restrictions—The part of net assets of a not-for-profit entity that is not subject to donor-imposed restrictions (donors include other types of contributors, including makers of certain grants

Statement of Financial Position (continued)

NOT-FOR-PROFIT COMPANY
STATEMENT OF FINANCIAL POSITION
DECEMBER 31, 20X2

Assets:

		Liabilities:	
Cash	100	Accounts payable	50
Marketable securities	300	Notes payable	100
Accounts receivable, net	40	Bonds payable	100
Inventory	120	Total liabilities	250
Property, plant, and equipment	80	**Net assets:**	
Total assets	640	Without donor restrictions	45
		With donor restrictions	345
		Total net assets	390
		Total liabilities and net assets	640

Statement of Activities

Similar to income statement:

- Reports revenues, gains, expenses, and losses
- Also reports net assets released from restrictions
- Categorized activities among net assets without donor restrictions and net assets with donor restrictions to provide change in net assets for each
- Change added to beginning balance to provide ending net assets for each category

Statement of Activities (continued)

	Total	Without Donor Restrictions	With Donor Restrictions
Revenues and gains			
Donations	665	265	400
Investment income	10	10	
Total revenues and gains	675	275	400
Net assets released from restriction			
Research restrictions		100	(100)
Time restrictions			
Property restrictions	—	20	(20)
Total net assets released from restriction	—	120	(120)

Statement of Activities (continued)

	Total	Without Donor Restrictions	With Donor Restrictions
Expenses and losses			
Depreciation	(10)	(10)	
Program expenses	(190)	(190)	
General and administrative	(85)	(85)	
Salaries	(70)	(70)	
Total expenses and losses	(355)	(355)	
Change in net assets	320	40	280
Net assets at December 31, 20X1	70	5	65
Net assets at December 31, 20X2	390	45	345

Statement of Cash Flows for Not-for-Profit Organizations

Similar to statement of cash flows under GAAP

- If the direct method is used, a reconciliation to the indirect method may be reported but is not required

Reporting Expenses by Nature and Function

All NFPs report information about all expenses in one location either:

- On the face of the statement of activities
- As a schedule in the notes to financial statements, or
- In a separate financial statement

The relationship between functional classification and natural classification for all expenses is presented in an analysis that disaggregates into functional expense classifications:

- Major classes of program services
- Supporting activities
- Natural expense classifications

Contributions Made to and Received by Not-for-Profit Organizations

In general, contributions are income to a not-for-profit organization

- Those that are part of the major, ongoing, and central operations are revenues
- Those that are not are gains

Without donor restrictions:

Cash	xxx	
Donations (without donor restrictions)		xxx

With donor restrictions:

Cash	xxx	
Donations (with donor restrictions)		xxx

Contributions Made to and Received by Not-for-Profit Organizations (continued)

Donated services:

Program expense (fair market value)	xxx	
Donations (without donor restrictions)		xxx

Cash donations with donor restrictions:

When made:

Cash	xxx	
Donations (with donor restrictions)		xxx

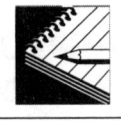

Contributions Made to and Received by Not-for-Profit Organizations (continued)

When used:

Net assets with donor restrictions	xxx	
Net assets without donor restrictions		xxx
Expense	xxx	
Cash		xxx

Unless donor stipulations limit the use of the assets for a period of time or for a particular purpose, donor restrictions on long-lived assets, if any, or cash to acquire or construct long-lived assets are considered to have expired when the assets are placed in service.

Pledges

Promises by outside parties to donate assets

- Recognized in period of pledge
- Allowance for uncollectible amount established
- Some or all may have time restriction with donor restriction
- Some or all may be without donor restriction

Pledges	xxx	
Allowance for uncollectible pledges		xxx
Donations (without donor restriction)		xxx
Donations (with donor restriction)		xxx

Other Donations

Donations of art, antiques, or artifacts not recognized if:

- Asset held for research or exhibition
- Asset preserved and unaltered
- Proceeds from sale of asset to be used to buy additional art, antiques, and artifacts

Donated assets to be held in trust

- Not recognized by not-for-profit organization
- Disclosed in footnotes to financial statements

SPECIAL INDUSTRIES: HEALTH CARE AND COLLEGES

Hospital Revenues

Patient service revenue recorded net of the allowance for patient bad debts

- Billing may be less due to Medicare allowance or employee discount
- Difference recorded in allowance account, including estimated bad debts from patients
- Statement of activities will report net amount

Services provided for free due to charity not recognized as revenues

Special transactions:

- Miscellaneous revenues from cafeteria, gift shop, parking lot fees, and educational programs classified as other revenue
- Donated supplies reported as operating revenue and expense when used
- Donations of essential services and donations without donor restrictions are nonoperating revenues

College Tuition Revenues

Students may receive refunds or price breaks

Refunds to students reduce tuition revenues

Price breaks may result from scholarships or reductions for family members of faculty or staff

- Tuition recognized at gross amount
- Price break recognized as expense

STATE AND LOCAL GOVERNMENT CONCEPTS

Governmental Accounting and Standards Board (GASB) Concepts Statements set forth fundamentals on which governmental accounting and reporting standards will be based

Purpose of financial reporting

- Accountability—Based on the belief that the taxpayer has a "right to know"
- Interperiod equity—Current period expenditures financed with current revenues

Concepts Statement No. 1 identified three primary users of the external state and local governmental financial reports

1. The citizenry
2. Legislative and oversight bodies
3. Investors and creditors

State and Local Government Concepts (continued)

Objective of Governmental Accounting

- Demonstrate and communicate compliance with the legal authorization to expend
- Assess service efforts and accomplishments of the governmental entity
- Demonstrate **interperiod equity**—Current period expenditures financed with current revenues

To demonstrate full accountability for all activities, information must include:

- Cost of services
- Sufficiency of revenues for services provided
- Financial position

The Concepts Statements encourage service efforts and Accomplishments (SEA) reporting

- Service efforts—Amount of financial and nonfinancial resources applied to a service
- Service accomplishments—Report what was achieved with resources used

Governmental Accounting Concepts

- Financial reporting—Governmental entities produce two distinct sets of financial statements: the fund statements and the government-wide (or entity-wide) statements
- Fund accounting—Governmental entities use funds to segregate resources by type of restriction
- Budgetary accounts provide control over expenditures
- Funds—A separate fiscal and accounting entity with a self-balancing sets of accounts—three categories:
  1. Governmental—Accounts for sources, uses, and balances of general government financial resources (e.g. taxes)
  2. Proprietary—Accounts for business-type activities
  3. Fiduciary—Accounts for resources held by a government in its capacity as trustee or agent for the benefit of others

Fund Types

Governmental funds (sometimes referred to as the "general government") include:

- General fund
- Special revenue funds
- Capital projects funds
- Debt service funds
- Permanent funds

Proprietary funds include:

- Enterprise funds
- Internal service funds

Fiduciary funds include:

- Pension and other employee benefit trust funds
- Investment trust funds
- Private purpose trust funds
- Agency funds

Measurement Focus Basis of Accounting

The basis of accounting defines the way in which inflows and outflows of resources are measured and recognized. In governmental accounting, the basis of accounting used varies depending on (1) the fund that is used to record the transaction and (2) the report that displays the transaction results.

Methods of Accounting

Funds of a governmental unit use two methods of accounting

1. Governmental funds use **modified accrual accounting**
2. Proprietary and fiduciary funds use accrual accounting

Modified Accrual Accounting

Differs from accrual accounting:

- Focus of financial reporting is financial position and flow of resources
- Revenues are recognized when they become available and measurable
- Expenditures are recorded when incurred or due to be paid from currently available resources in the governmental fund

Budgetary Accounting

Budgetary accounting requires the creation of special budgetary accounts, recording of budgetary entries, and preparation of reports that compare budget amounts to actual amounts.

Reporting on budgetary results is required for:

- General fund *and*
- Each major annually budgeted special revenue fund (based on quantitative results)

Optional Reporting Placement

- As part of basic fund-level financial statements
- As part of required supplementary information after the notes to the financial statements

Encumbrance Accounting

To ensure that the entity does not order more goods than it has the authority to purchase, an estimate of expenditures is recorded at the time an order is placed rather than waiting until the goods are received.

The unexpended, unencumbered appropriation is the remaining authorization to spend after taking into account goods still on order (encumbrances) and goods received to date (expenditures). Synonymous terms include: uncommitted appropriations, available balance, unencumbered balance, and free balance. This balance is calculated as

+ Appropriations
− Encumbrances
− Expenditures
= Unencumbered, unexpended appropriation

Beginning of Year

Governmental unit adopts annual budget for general fund

Budget recorded with following entry:

Estimated revenues	xxx		
Estimated other financing sources	xxx		
Budgetary fund balance	xxx	or	xxx
Appropriations			xxx
Estimated other financing uses			xxx

Estimated revenues = Revenues expected to be collected during the year

Estimated other financing sources = Estimate of proceeds from bond issues and operating transfers in

Budgetary fund balance (plug) = Amount required to balance the entry

Appropriations = Authorized spending (planned expenditures)

Estimated other financing uses = Expected operating transfers out (e.g., interfund transfers, proceeds from bonds)

During the Year

Revenue cycle consists of billing certain revenues, such as property taxes, collecting billed revenues, writing off uncollectible billings, and collecting unbilled revenues

Billing of revenues:

Taxes receivable	xxx	
Allowance for estimated uncollectible taxes		xxx
Deferred revenues		xxx
Revenues control		xxx

Taxes receivable = Amount billed

Allowance for estimated uncollectible taxes = Billings expected to be uncollectible

- This amount may be adjusted upward or downward during the year
- Offsetting entry will be to revenues control

Deferred revenues = Portion of billed taxes expected to be collected more than 60 days after close of current year

During the Year (continued)

Revenues control = Portion of billed taxes expected to be collected during the current year or within 60 days of close

Collecting billed revenues:

Cash	xxx	
Taxes receivable		xxx

Writing off uncollectible amounts:

Allowance for estimated uncollectible taxes	xxx	
Taxes receivable		xxx

Collecting unbilled revenues:

Cash	xxx	
Revenues control		xxx

During the Year (continued)

Spending cycle consists of ordering goods and services, receiving the goods and services, and paying for them

Ordering goods and services:

Encumbrances control (estimated cost)	xxx	
Budgetary fund balance assigned		xxx

Receiving goods and services:

Budgetary fund balance reserved for encumbrances (estimated cost)	xxx	
Encumbrances control		xxx
Expenditures control (actual cost)	xxx	
Vouchers payable		xxx

During the Year (continued)

Payment:

Vouchers payable	xxx	
Cash		xxx

Other financing sources and uses are recorded as the transactions occur:

- Proceeds of long-term debit issues are recorded as other financing sources when received
- Operating transfers to or from other funds are reported as other financing uses or sources as the funds are transferred

Adjustments at Balance Sheet Date

Closing entry—Eliminating revenues, expenditures, and encumbrances:

Revenues control	xxx		
Fund balance (plug)	xxx	or	xxx
Expenditures control			xxx
Encumbrances control			xxx

Close outstanding encumbrances at year end:

Budgetary fund balance	xxx	
Encumbrances		xxx
Fund balance—unassigned	xxx	
Fund balance—assigned		xxx

End of Year

Budget recorded in beginning of year is reversed:

Appropriations	xxx		
Estimated other financing uses	xxx		
Budgetary fund balance	xxx	or	xxx
Estimated revenues control			xxx
Estimated other financing sources			xxx

Beginning of the Next Year

Opening entry at the beginning of the next year:

Encumbrances—Prior year	xxx	
Budgetary fund balance		xxx
Fund balance—Assigned	xxx	
Fund balance—Unassigned		xxx

Deferred Outflows and Deferred Inflows of Resources

Unlike revenues and expenses, which are inflows and outflows of resources related to the period in which they occur, deferred outflows and deferred inflows of resources are related to future periods. Recognition of deferred inflows or revenues and expenses is deferred until the future period to which the inflows and outflows are related.

GASB Concepts Statement No. 4 stipulates that recognition of deferred outflows and deferred inflows is limited to those items identified by GASB.

Net Position

Net position represents the difference between assets and liabilities in government-wide financial statements (GASB Concepts Statement No. 34) and in fund-level financial statements for proprietary fund types and fiduciary fund types

- Assets + Deferred outflows of resources – Liabilities – Deferred inflows of resources = Net position

Three categories of net position:

1. **Net assets invested in capital assets, net of related debt**—All capital assets, including restricted assets, net of depreciation and reduced by related debt
2. **Restricted net position**—Items with externally imposed restrictions on use distinguishing major categories of restrictions
3. **Unrestricted net position**—Remainder

Caution: Board-designated funds are part of unrestricted net position

Fund Balance

Equity section account for governmental fund types

Governmental Fund Balance Classifications

- Nonspendable (e.g., inventory or permanent endowment)
- Spendable (four classifications)
    - Restricted fund balance (restricted either by contributor or law)
    - Committed fund balance (committed to specific purposes by highest level of governmental decision-making authority)
    - Assigned fund balance (amounts intended for specific purposes that are not classified as restricted or committed but not bound to unassigned)
    - Unassigned fund balance (residual classification for amounts not classified as restricted, committed, or assigned)

Governmental Funds

- Modified accrual accounting
- Revenue recognition
- "Expenditures" not "expenses"
- Fund balance—five categories
- Balance sheet, statement of revenues, expenditures and changes in fund balance, and revenues, expenditures, and changes in fund balance—budget-to-actual

A governmental unit maintains five types of governmental funds:

1. General fund—All activities not accounted for in another fund

   - Only fund that reports positive unassigned fund balance

Governmental Funds (continued)

2. Special revenue funds—Account for revenues earmarked to finance specific activities other than debt service or capital projects

3. Capital projects funds—Account for monies designated for acquisition or construction of significant capital items (i.e. buildings, equipment)

4. Debt service fund—Account for monies set aside for payment of general obligation debts of other governmental funds (does not account for the liability itself, only for monies set aside)

5. Permanent funds—Account for resources that are legally restricted

   - Fixed assets and long-term debt not reported in governmental funds
   - Instead, reported in government-wide financial statements

General Fund Accounting

A governmental unit will have one general fund

- Annual budget is recorded at the beginning of the year
- Revenues, expenditures, and other financing sources and uses are recorded during the year
- Adjustments are made at the balance sheet date
- Budgetary accounts are closed at year-end
- Accounts for current items only

Special Revenue Fund

Used to account for monies restricted or "earmarked" for specific types of general government expenditures

- Accounting identical to general fund

Capital Projects Fund

Used to account for major capital projects

- Fund opened when project commences and closed when project complete
- Accounting similar to general fund

Differences in accounting for capital projects fund:

1. Budgetary entries generally not made
2. Expenditures generally made under contract
   - Credit contracts payable
   - Credit retention payable for deferred payments

Debt Service Fund

Used to account for funds accumulated to make principal and interest payments on general obligation debts

- Expenditures include principal and interest payable in current period
- Resources consist of amounts transferred from other funds (other financing sources) and earnings on investments (revenues)

Amounts used for interest payments separated from amounts used for principal payments

Cash for interest	xxx	
Cash for principal	xxx	
Other financing sources		xxx

Proprietary Funds

Account for governmental activities conducted similarly to business enterprises

- Uses accrual basis accounting
- "Expenses" rather than expenditures
- Long term debt, fixed assets, and depreciation expense
- Net position—Three categories: Net investment in capital assets, restricted, and unrestricted

Enterprise fund:

- Used to account for business-type activities to the general public
- Earned income recognized as operating revenues
- Shared taxes reported as nonoperating revenues

Internal service fund:

- Used to account for services provided to other governmental departments on a fee or cost-reimbursement basis
- Resources come from billings to other funds
- Reported as operating revenues

Fiduciary Funds

- Accrual accounting
- Excluded from government-wide financial statements
- Fund-level financial statements: Statement of fiduciary net position, statement of changes in fiduciary net position (uses addition and deductions), and restricted net position

Pension Trust Fund

Accounts for assets held in trust for employees, retirees, and beneficiaries of pension plans

Additional information in notes and supplementary information following notes includes:

- Schedule of funding progress
- Schedule of employer contributions
- Actuarial information
- Components of the pension liability
- Significant assumptions to measure the pension liability
- 10-year schedules of changes in pension liability

Investment Trust Fund

Accounts for assets received from other governments units to be invested on their behalf.

Private Purpose Trust Fund

Accounts for resources held on behalf of private persons or organizations.

- Does not include resources for pension plans, investment pools, or permanent funds

Agency Fund

Accounts for money collected for various funds, other governments, or outsiders

- No equity
- Current assets = Current liabilities

FORMAT AND CONTENT OF COMPREHENSIVE ANNUAL FINANCIAL REPORT (CAFR)

The Comprehensive Annual Financial Report

GASB specifies two levels of reporting for governmental entities: the general purpose financial statements and the comprehensive annual financial report (CAFR)

CAFR—Three sections:
1. Introduction section
2. Financial
   - Auditor's report
   - Management's discussion and analysis (MD&A)
   - Government-wide statements
   - Fund statements
   - Notes to the financial statements
   - Required supplementary information (RSI)
3. Statistical

Management Discussion and Analysis (MD&A)

Purpose is to help the user assess the overall financial condition of the governmental entity and determine whether the government's position has improved or deteriorated during the period

Should include:

- Condensed comparison of current-year financial information to prior year
- Analysis of overall financial position and results of operations
- Analysis of balances and transactions in individual funds
- Analysis of significant budget variances
- Description of capital assets and long-term debt activity during the period
- Currently known facts, decisions, or conditions expected to affect financial position or results of operations; forecasts or subjective information not permitted

Government-Wide Financial Statements

Consist of:

- Statement of net position
- Statement of activities

Report on overall government

- Do not display information about individual funds
- Exclude fiduciary activities or component units that are fiduciary
- Distinction made between primary government and discretely presented component units
- Distinction made between government-type activities and business-type activities of primary government
- Internal service funds (ISF) are not reported in the government-wide financial statements; rather, the amounts in the ISF are blended into governmental activities and business activities according to the use by each of the ISF services
- Business-type activities include enterprise funds only

Characteristics of Government-Wide Financial Statements

Use economic measurement focus for all assets, liabilities, revenues, expenses, gains, and losses

Apply accrual basis of accounting

Revenues from exchanges or exchange-like transactions recognized in period of exchange

Revenues from nonexchange transactions:

- **Derived tax revenues** imposed on exchange transactions recognized as asset and revenues when exchange occurs
- **Imposed tax revenues** imposed on nongovernment agencies recognized as asset when government has enforceable claim and as revenues when use of resources required or permitted
- **Government-mandated nonexchange transactions** provided by one level of government for another recognized as asset and revenue (or liability and expense) when all eligibility requirements met
- **Voluntary nonexchange transactions** recognized similarly to government-mandated nonexchange transactions

Statement of Net Position—Government-Wide Financial Statements

- Assets and liabilities in order of liquidity/maturity
- Assets include both current and fixed assets
- Current and noncurrent portions of liabilities reported
- Assets + Deferred outflows of resources − Liabilities − Deferred inflows of resources = Net position

Assets, deferred outflows of resources, liabilities, deferred inflows of resources, and net position reported for primary government

- Separate columns for government-type activities and business-type activities
- Amounts combined in total column

Assets, deferred outflows of resources, liabilities, deferred inflows of resources, and net position also reported for component units

- Amounts reported similarly as those for primary government
- Column **not** combined with totals for primary government

Focus on

Format and Content of Comprehensive Annual Financial Report (CAFR)   **318**

Statement of Activities—Government-Wide Financial Statements

Self-financing activities distinguished from those drawing from general revenues

For each government function:

- Net expense or revenue
- Relative burden

Governmental activities presented by function

Business-type activities presented by business segment

Items reported separately after net expenses of government's functions:

- General revenues
- Contributions to term and permanent endowments
- Contributions to permanent fund principal
- Special items—those that are unusual **or** infrequent
- Extraordinary items—those that are unusual **and** infrequent
- Transfers

Focus on

Format and Content of Comprehensive Annual Financial Report (CAFR)   **319**

Items on Statement of Activities

Depreciation—Indirect expense charged to function with asset

- Allocated among functions for shared assets
- Not required to be allocated to functions for general capital assets
- Not allocated to functions for eligible general infrastructure assets

  - Government uses an asset management system
  - Government documents assets preserved appropriately

Revenues classified into categories:

- Amounts received from users or beneficiaries of a program always **program revenues**
- Amounts received from parties outside citizenry are **general revenues** if unrestricted or program revenues if restricted to specific programs
- Amounts received from taxpayers always general revenues
- Amounts generated by the government usually general revenues
- Contributions to term and permanent endowments, contributions to permanent fund principal, special and extraordinary items, and transfers reported separately

Format of Statement of Activities

Information for each program or function reported separately:

- Expenses
- Charges for services
- Operating grants and contributions
- Capital grants and contributions

Difference between expenses and revenues reported for each program:

- Equal to change in net position
- Separated into columns for governmental activities and business-type activities
- Combined into a total column

Remaining items (general revenues, grants and contributions, special and extraordinary items, and transfers) reported separately below functions and programs:

- Divided into governmental activities and business-type activities with total column
- Provides change in net position and ending net position with same amounts as statement of net position
- Separate column for component units not combined into total

Additional Characteristics of Government-Wide Financial Statements

Internal amounts

- Eliminated to avoid doubling up
- Interfund receivables and payables eliminated
- Amounts due between government-type and business-type activities presented as offsetting internal balances

Capital assets include the following:

- Land, land improvements, and easements
- Buildings and building improvements
- Vehicles, machinery, and equipment
- Works of art and historical treasures
- Infrastructure

Additional Characteristics of Government-Wide Financial Statements (continued)

- All other tangible and intangible assets with initial useful lives greater than a single period
  - Only identifiable intangibles
  - Internally generated intangibles begin to be capitalized if
    - Objective and capacity identified
    - Feasible
    - Intent to complete
- Pension plans
  - **Single-employer defined benefit plan** or **agent defined benefit plan**
    - Reports a net pension liability, which is measured as the portion of the actuarial present value of projected benefit payments attributable to past periods of employee service minus the pension plan's fiduciary net position

Determining the Financial Reporting Entity

A **component unit** is a legally separate organization for which the elected officials of a primary government are financially accountable.

Users should be able to distinguish between primary government and component units—Component units may be **blended** when:

- Governing body of component is essentially the same as that of the primary government
- The component provides services almost exclusively for the primary government
- The component unit's total debt outstanding, including leases, is expected to be repaid entirely or almost entirely by the primary government

Most component units will be **discretely presented.**

Financial Statements of Governmental Funds

Statements of governmental funds

- Balance sheet (five categories of fund balance)
- Statement of revenues, expenditures, and changes in fund balances

Focus is to report sources, uses, and balances of current financial resources

- Apply modified accrual accounting
- Capital assets and long-term debt not reported as assets or liabilities

Reports include separate columns for each major governmental fund and single column for total of all nonmajor funds:

- General fund is always major
- Others major if assets, liabilities, revenues, expenditures meet the 5% and 10% tests:
  - Fund at least 5% of *total* column in government-wide financial statements
  - Fund at least 10% of *government-type* column in government-wide financial statements

Balance Sheet

Reports assets, liabilities, and fund balances

- Reported separately for each major governmental fund

Total fund balances reconciled to net position of governmental activities in government-wide financial statements

Statement of Revenues, Expenditures, and Changes in Fund Balances

Reports inflows, outflows, and balances of current financial resources

- Reported separately for each major governmental fund
- Revenues classified by major source
- Expenditures classified by function

Statement of Revenues, Expenditures, and Changes in Fund Balances (continued)

Format of statement:

Revenues

<u>– Expenditures</u>

= Excess (deficiency) of revenues over expenditures

± Other financing sources and uses

<u>± Special and extraordinary items</u>

= Net change in fund balances

<u>+ Fund balances—beginning of period</u>

= Fund balances—end of period

Change in fund balances reconciled to change in net position of governmental activities in government-wide financial statements

Financial Statements of Proprietary Funds

Statements of proprietary funds

- Statement of net position
- Statement of revenues, expenses, and changes in net position
- Statement of cash flows

Preparation of statements

- Emphasis is measurement of economic resources
- Prepared under accrual basis of accounting
- Reports include separate column for each enterprise fund meeting 5% and 10% tests:
  - Fund at least 5% of *total* column in government-wide financial statements
  - Fund at least 10% of *business-type* column in government-wide financial statements
  - Total of nonmajor enterprise funds in a single column
  - Total of all internal service funds in a single column

Financial Statements of Proprietary Funds (continued)

- Four categories—Statement of cash flows

   1. Operating
   2. Noncapital financing
   3. Capital and related financing
   4. Investing

- Derivatives: Reported at fair value
- Evaluated for effectiveness each financial reporting period
- Land held for investment reported at fair value

Statement of Net Position

Prepared in classified format

- Current and noncurrent assets and liabilities distinguished
- Net position reported in same categories as used in government-wide financial statements

Statement of Revenues, Expenses, and Changes in Fund Net Position

Amounts should be the same as net position and changes in net position shown for business-type activities in government-wide financial statements

- Revenues reported by major source
- Operating and nonoperating revenues and expenses distinguished
- Nonoperating revenues and expenses reported after operating income

Statement of Revenues, Expenses, and Changes in Fund Net Position (continued)

Format of Statement of Revenues, Expenses, and Changes in Fund Net Position

Operating revenues (listed by source)

−   Operating expenses (listed by category)

=   Operating income or loss

±   Nonoperating revenues and expenses

=   Income before other revenues, expenses, gains, losses, and transfers

±   Capital contributions, additions to permanent and term endowments, special and extraordinary items, and transfers

=   Increase or decrease in net position

+   Net position—beginning of period

=   Net position—end of period

Statement of Cash Flows

Shows sources and uses of cash by major classification

- Operating activities reported using direct method
- Noncapital financing activities
- Capital and related financing activities
- Investing activities

Operating income reconciled to cash flows from operating activities (indirect method)

Financial Statements of Fiduciary Funds

Statements of fiduciary funds

- Statement of fiduciary net position
- Statement of changes in fiduciary net position

Focus of fiduciary financial statements:

- Emphasis on measurement of economic resources
- Prepared using accrual basis of accounting

Report includes separate column for each major fiduciary fund and column for total of all non-major fiduciary funds.

- Selection of major funds based on judgment of entity management
- No 5% and 10% tests since fiduciary funds weren't included in government-wide financial statements

Notes to Government-Wide Financial Statements

Intended to provide information needed for fair presentation of financial statements

Notes include:

- Summary of significant accounting policies
- Disclosure about capital assets and long-term liabilities
- Disclosure about major classes of capital assets
- Disclosure about donor-restricted endowments
- Budgetary basis of accounting

Required Supplementary Information

Presented in addition to MD&A

Consists of:

- Budgetary comparison schedules for governmental funds
- Pension plan and other postemployment benefit (OPEB) plan disclosures
- Combining financial statements and individual fund financial statements
- Information about infrastructure reported under the modified approach

TYPICAL ITEMS AND SPECIFIC TYPES OF TRANSACTIONS AND EVENTS

Interfund Transactions

Nonreciprocal transfers are transfers of resources from one fund to another without any receipts of goods or services, such as a transfer of money from the general fund to a capital projects fund.

Paying fund:

Other financing uses/sources control	xxx	
Cash		xxx

Receiving fund:

Cash	xxx	
Other financing uses/sources control		xxx

Interfund Transactions (continued)

Reciprocal transfers (quasi-external) occur when one fund acquires goods or services from another in a transaction similar to one that would occur with outsiders.

Paying fund:

Expenditures control **or** Expenses	xxx	
Due to fund		xxx

Receiving fund:

Due from fund	xxx	
Revenues control		xxx

When the amounts are paid in cash, the liability/receivable is eliminated in each of the funds.

Interfund Transactions (continued)

Reimbursements occur when one fund makes payments on behalf of another fund. These transactions reimburse one fund for expenditures that should have been recorded in another fund. They are recorded as an expense or expenditure in the fund making the reimbursement and as a reduction in expense or expenditure (not a revenue) in the fund that is reimbursed.

When a fund has previously paid for an expenditure/expense on behalf of another the journal entry to record the reimbursement is:

Reimbursing fund:

Expenditures control **or** Expenses	xxx	
Cash		xxx

Receiving fund:

Cash	xxx	
Expenditures control **or** Expenses		xxx

Interfund Transactions (continued)

Loans may be made from one fund to another

Lending fund:

       Due from/Advance to other fund (fund identified)*   xxx
         Cash   xxx

Receiving fund:

      Cash   xxx
        Due to/Advances from other fund (fund identified)*   xxx

*Due/from to denotes short-term debt; Advance to/from from indicates long-term debt

Accounting for Capital Assets and Infrastructure

Capital assets reported at historical cost

- Includes capitalized interest and costs of getting asset ready for intended use
- Depreciated over useful lives
- Inexhaustible assets not depreciated
- Infrastructure assets may be depreciated under modified approach

Infrastructure includes:

- Capital assets with longer lives than most capital assets that are normally stationary
- Roads, bridges, tunnels, drainage systems, water and sewer systems, dams, and lighting systems

Eligible infrastructure assets not depreciated

- Must be part of network or subsystem maintained and preserved at established condition levels
- Additions and improvements increasing capacity or efficiency capitalized
- Other expenditures expensed

Solid Waste Landfill Operations

The Environmental Protection Agency imposes requirements on solid waste landfills

- Procedures for closures
- Procedures for postclosure care

Procedures represent long-term obligations accounted for as long-term debt

- Costs to be incurred by governmental funds accounted for in general long-term debt account group
- Expenditures in governmental funds reduce general long-term debt account group balances
- Costs to be incurred by proprietary funds accounted for directly in funds
- Costs associated with closure and postclosure procedures accounted for during periods of operation

INDEX